D0296174

THE BOOK OF
Greek
COOKING

VALE OF LEVEN ACADEMY
LIBRARY

THE BOOK OF
Greek
COOKING

LESLEY MACKLEY

Photographed by
JON STEWART

PUBLISHED BY
SALAMANDER BOOKS LIMITED
LONDON

Published by Salamander Books Limited
8 Blenheim Court, Brewery Road, London N7 9NT

© Salamander Books Ltd., 1993, 2000

ISBN 1 84065 271 3

A member of the Chrysalis Group plc

All rights reserved. Except for use in a review, no part
of this book may be reproduced, stored in a retrieval
system or transmitted by any means, electronic, mechanical,
photocopying, recording or otherwise, without prior
permission of Salamander Books Ltd.

Managing Editor: Felicity Jackson
Art Director: Roger Daniels
Photographer: Jon Stewart, assisted by Sandra Lambell and Nicole Mai
Home Economists: Kerenza Harries and Jo Craig
Typeset by: BMD Graphics, Hemel Hempstead
Colour separation by: Scantrans Pte. Ltd, Singapore
Printed and bound in Spain

ACKNOWLEDGEMENTS

The Publishers would like to thank the following for their
help and advice:
Barbara Stewart at Prop Exchange, Unit F,
51 Calthorpe Street, London WC1.

Notes:
All spoon measurements are equal.
1 teaspoon = 5 ml spoon
1 tablespoon = 15 ml spoon.

CONTENTS

INTRODUCTION

The custom of serving small snacks with drinks is widespread throughout the Mediterranean countries. In Greece these snacks, or mezes, can take the form of anything from small nibbles such as olives or pickled peppers (capsicums) served with a glass of ouzo, to a selection of different dishes which make up a more substantial meal.

The first section of this book contains a wide variety of dishes for serving as mezes, but many of the other recipes could be served in smaller quantities as part of a meze selection. Similarly, many of the meze recipes could be increased to make a main course, starter or vegetable accompaniment.

With over 100 beautifully illustrated recipes, this book brings you the full range and variety of Greek cooking, something not always apparent to the casual visitor. There are dishes for every occasion – for entertaining, family meals, buffets and drinks parties – plus a whole selection of recipes suitable for vegetarians. Some are familiar favourites (sometimes adapted for modern tastes) and others may be less well known, but all are guaranteed to put a little Mediterranean sunshine into your menus!

GREEK COOKING

Greek food is simple, colourful and packed with robust flavours. Although many dishes show influences from Greece's past, particularly Arab, Turkish and Italian, they have a distinctive style of their own; a style which has changed little over the years. Greece has a long tradition of fine cooking and the full range of delicious Greek dishes often remains undiscovered by the holidaymaker.

THE GREEK DIET
The Greek diet, like that of other countries around the Mediterranean, is extremely healthy, being low in processed foods and animal fats and is based on the availability of local produce: wheat products such as bread, pastry and pasta, fresh fruit and vegetables, fish and olive oil.

MEAT
Meat does not have the significance it has in Britain, America or Australia as it has always been a comparative luxury. Greece does not have the lush pastures needed to support large herds of cattle, but both sheep and goats can survive on quite poor land.

These hardy animals produce somewhat tougher and better flavoured meat than we are used to, but the Greeks make imaginative use of it in recipes which make a small amount of meat go a long way. Stews are given long slow cooking until the meat is beautifully tender, and many recipes require the meat to be marinated before cooking which also helps to tenderise it. Little beef is eaten and it is usually cut into cubes for kebabs or minced.

No part of the animal is wasted and offal is used imaginatively in many recipes. For festivals and special occasions, a whole lamb will be rubbed with olive oil, stuffed with herbs and roasted on a spit over a charcoal filled pit, filling the air with the aroma of woodsmoke, herbs and roasting meat.

Traditional Greek recipes give cooking times for meat which result in it practically falling apart, therefore the cooking times given in this book have taken into account the better quality of the meat which will be used.

POULTRY
The first mention of poultry keeping in Europe is in a Greek reference in 570 B.C. and chicken and other poultry, and game, are as popular as ever. Guinea fowl, partridge and quail all appear in many traditional recipes.

DAIRY PRODUCE
Sheep and goats are traditionally the main dairy animals in Greece, but nowadays much of the milk used is cows' milk. Milk is not used much as a drink mainly because, in the days before refrigeration, it did not keep in the warm climate and had to be made into a longer lasting product such as cheese or yogurt.

Cows', goats' and sheeps' milk are all made into cheese and yogurt. Sheeps' milk contains more fat and protein than cows' or goats' milk and makes a particularly thick rich yogurt and some excellent cheeses.

Traditionally, butter is not used much in Greek cooking as olive oil is favoured as a cooking medium, giving a distinctive Mediterranean flavour to many dishes.

FISH
As the Greek mainland is almost surrounded by sea and much of the country is made up of hundreds of islands, fish naturally plays a very important part in the diet.

The seas are rich with a wide variety of fish all the year round. Red and grey mullet are very popular and turbot, bass, sea bream, swordfish and halibut are also widely used.

Octopus is beaten against the stones on the beach to tenderise it, then it is fried, grilled or cooked in a sauce, as is squid. Crab, mussels, prawns and lobster are also excellent.

The most popular method of cooking fish is grilling, but it is also frequently cooked in a tomato sauce. Taramasalta is made from smoked fish roe. Originally the roe of the grey mullet was used, but nowadays it is more likely to be cod's roe. Fish soups are popular; it is thought that the well-known Provencal bouillabaisse developed from the Greek kakavia.

VEGETABLES
Vegetables grow well in the sunny climate and are a very important part of the Greek diet. Vegetables are not necessarily considered an accompaniment to meat, but feature in special dishes on their own, or in combinations.

As in all the Mediterranean countries, peppers (capsicums), tomatoes, courgettes (zucchini), aubergines (eggplants), onions and garlic grow in abundance and feature in many recipes but other popular vegetables include horta (similar to spinach), spinach, artichokes, broad beans, green beans, cabbage, fennel, leeks and okra.

Many beans are dried for use in the winter, broad beans, chick peas, haricot beans and kidney beans being amongst the most widely used. They are soaked, then cooked, sometimes with other vegetables or in a tomato sauce, or they may be made into a purée or dip, or used in a salad, often combined in a three-bean salad.

FRUIT
Fruit also grows in abundance in the hot sunny climate and market stalls are piled with an enormous variety. Citrus fruits grow well and lemons are particu-

larly important in Greek cuisine, being used to flavour everything from soups and sauces to cakes and pastries. Apricots, cherries, dates, figs, grapes, melons, peaches, plums and pomegranates are among the many fruits which flourish, but there are also some more 'old fashioned' fruits such as quinces and medlars which are also very popular.

Apricots, dates, figs and peaches are among those which are dried, and all sorts of fruits are also preserved in syrup and served to guests in a small dish accompanied by a glass of water.

The most important fruit grown in Greece is the olive, and the olive tree and its fruit has always been central to the daily lives of the Greeks. Not only the fruit and oil are used but the beautiful grained wood is made into furniture. Nuts are widely used in Greek cooking, particularly almonds, pine nuts, pistachio nuts and walnuts.

PASTA, RICE AND BREAD

Although pasta does not have the significance it has in Italy, it is very popular in Greece, and spaghetti, macaroni and orzo, particularly, often appear on the menu.

The Greeks learnt breadmaking from the Egyptians and, as in all Mediterranean countries, it is still extremely important. A wide variety of loaves and rolls can be seen in any baker's shop, from flat pitta bread to elaborately braided loaves. There are several traditional breads which are made for special festivals.

Rice is grown in Greece and is an important item in the Greek diet. It is used in both sweet and savoury dishes.

SWEET DISHES

Although many of the Greek pastries, cakes and desserts are extremely sweet, often dripping with syrup or honey, the overall sugar consumption is half that of Britain or the U.S.A. Sweet dishes are reserved for special occasions.

EATING PATTERNS

A typical day's eating pattern begins early with a breakfast consisting of bread and olive oil with feta cheese and olives. On cold mornings in more mountainous regions, farm workers eat a large hot breakfast before going out to work on the land.

Nowadays, people living in the cities and working in offices generally have bread or toast with marmalade and butter, but they may also have tomatoes, olives, cheese or salami.

Lunch may be eaten any time between noon and 3 p.m. It may be simply a dish of beans and pulses, sometimes accompanied with salted herrings or sardines. Fried eggs with fried potatoes or chips is a popular lunch!

A salad is always served with lunch. In the summer it consists of lettuce with tomatoes and cucumber, often with olives, raw onion and feta cheese. In winter the salads are usually made with finely shredded cabbage dressed with olive oil and lemon or vinegar.

A glass of wine may be drunk with lunch it is usually followed by a 'siesta'! Lunch may be more substantial and could start with meze or soup. There is no general rule and habits change according to the season.

The evening meal may start with soup which is usually followed by fried fish or a meat dish and cooked vegetables or salad. Desserts are rarely eaten after an everyday meal as they tend to be associated with Sundays and feast days. Fruit is eaten but not necessarily after a meal; it may be a mid-afternoon snack accompanied by a small cup of black coffee.

STREET LIFE

The sociable temperament of the Greeks and the warm climate encourages street life and there are numerous cafés, milk bars and street stalls serving delicious snacks such as yogurts, ice creams, pastries and roast chestnuts. Pastry shops serve cakes and sweet pastries with drinks such as fruit nectars, lemonade or black coffee.

DRINKS

At home alcohol is rarely drunk on its own, but as an accompaniment to food and it is generally only served when entertaining. Sweet fruit drinks and mineral water are normally served with a meal. Greek hospitality is such that it is impossible to visit a Greek home without being offered something to drink, and a drink is never served without something to eat. Coffee might be accompanied by preserved fruits in syrup and other drinks will be served with anything from a few olives to a complete array of mezes.

POPULAR INGREDIENTS

Cheese: Feta cheese is a white, salty cheese stored in strong brine. It is traditionally made from unpasteurised ewes' milk but the imported feta cheese is generally made from cows' milk. It is most frequently used in salads but can also be used in cooked pastries. Cottage cheese can sometimes be used as a substitute. Kefalotiri is a strong cheese which is good for grating. Parmesan or a well-flavoured Cheddar may be used instead. Haloumi is a soft- to semi-soft goats' milk cheese which is quite salty and yet mild. It is generally served toasted or fried.

Tomatoes: Greek tomatoes are sweet and full of flavour. At times when our own tomatoes do not have much flavour it is preferable to use canned tomatoes. Even when using fresh tomatoes it may be necessary to add a little sugar to bring out the flavour.

Rigani: The dried leaves and flowers of a Mediterranean marjoram. It is sold in Greek delicatessens but is not widely available, so oregano has been used instead in the recipes here as it is closer to rigani than marjoram.

Olives: Greek olives come in all shapes, colours and sizes. The best known ones outside Greece are the sweet-sour Kalamata olives.

Olive oil: Many Greek recipes are given their distinctive flavour by the use of good quality olive oil. Where possible extra virgin olive oil should be used as it has the strongest flavour, but sometimes a less pronounced flavour is required and then refined olive oil or sunflower oil may be used.

Pine nuts: These are not really nuts but are kernels from cones of the stone pine. They are expensive, but have a very distinctive resinous flavour and there is really no substitute for them.

Orzo: A rice-shaped pasta which may be difficult to find outside specialist shops. Any other small or 'soup' pasta may be used, or even rice.

Honey: The finest Greek honey is the fragrant Hymettus honey, but no other flower honeys such as lavender or orange blossom may be substituted for it. If the recipe does not specify a fragrant honey a blended honey will give satisfactory results.

Yogurt: Where yogurt is used in recipes in this book, thick Greek yogurt – which is now widely available – should be used. Sheeps' or cows' milk yogurt may be used, although sheeps' milk yogurt is richer and creamier.

Filo pastry: Filo pastry is known as Phyllo in Greece. There are various makes of pastry available and they are not a standard size. The pastry used in the recipes in this book comes in long narrow packets containing 20-24 sheets, measuring approximately 30 x 50 cm (12 x 20 in). When handling filo pastry, it is important to keep the sheets in a pile covered with a damp cloth and work with one sheet at a time, layering it or filling it, otherwise the pastry will dry out.

Orange flower water: Many of the sweet dishes in this book contain orange flower water which gives a fragrant flavour to fruit dishes.

Rosewater: Like orange flower water, rosewater is used in many sweet dishes, particularly milk-based desserts. It should be labelled as 'triple distilled'. If it is bought from a chemist it may be mixed with glycerine.

—CHEESE & HERB TRIANGLES—

115 g (4 oz) feta cheese
115 g (4 oz) cottage cheese
½ egg, beaten
1 tablespoon chopped fresh parsley
1 tablespoon chopped fresh mint
1 tablespoon chopped fresh chives
pepper
4 sheets filo pastry
55 g (2 oz/¼ cup) butter

Crumble feta cheese into a bowl. Add cottage cheese, egg, parsley, mint, chives and pepper. Blend together with a fork.

Preheat oven to 190C (375F/Gas 5). Butter a baking sheet. Lay the sheets of filo in a pile on a work surface. Keep covered while working with one sheet at a time. In a small saucepan, melt butter. Brush one sheet of filo with butter. Cut it into 4 long strips.

Place a teaspoon of filling in one corner of filo strip. Fold a corner of pastry over filling. Turn triangle over and over to the end of the strip. Repeat with remaining pastry. Brush tops of triangles with butter. Bake in the oven for 10-12 minutes until crisp and brown.

Makes 16.

——MARINATED FETA CHEESE——

350 g (12 oz) feta cheese
2 cloves garlic
½ teaspoon mixed peppercorns
8 coriander seeds
1 bay leaf
oregano and thyme sprigs
olive oil to cover
hot toast, cut into squares, to serve

Cut feta cheese into cubes. Cut garlic into thick slivers.

In a mortar and pestle, lightly crush peppercorns and coriander seeds.

Pack cubes of cheese into a preserving jar with the bay leaf, interspersing layers of cheese with garlic, peppercorns, coriander and oregano or thyme. Pour in enough olive oil to cover cheese. Leave for 2 weeks. Serve on hot toast, sprinkled with a little of the oil from the jar.

Serves 6.

─────── HERB & FETA BALLS ───────

225 g (8 oz) cream cheese
85 g (3 oz) feta cheese
1 clove garlic, crushed
1 teaspoon chopped fresh parsley
1 teaspoon chopped fresh mint
6 teaspoons sesame seeds, 3 teaspoons finely chopped
    fresh parsley and 3 teaspoons finely chopped fresh
    mint, to garnish
vine leaves, to serve

In a bowl, mix together cream cheese and feta
cheese until smooth. Stir in garlic, parsley
and mint.

Roll cheese into 20 balls. Chill for at least 1
hour. Meanwhile, toast sesame seeds for
garnish. Put in a frying pan and heat until
seeds are golden brown, stirring frequently.
Leave to cool.

To serve, mix together chopped parsley
and chopped mint for garnish. Roll half
cheese balls in herbs and half in toasted
sesame seeds. Serve on vine leaves.

Makes 20.

SPANAKOPITTA

450 g (1 lb) frozen spinach
2 tablespoons olive oil
1 small onion, finely chopped
1 clove garlic, crushed
2 tablespoons chopped fresh coriander
½ teaspoon freshly grated nutmeg
115 g (4 oz) feta cheese, crumbled
1 egg, lightly beaten
salt and pepper
55 g (2 oz/¼ cup) butter
4 sheets filo pastry
coriander leaves, to garnish

Cook spinach according to packet instructions. Drain and chop.

Preheat oven to 180C (350F/Gas 4). Butter a 20 cm (8 in) square tin. In a small frying pan, heat oil, then add onion and garlic and cook until onion is soft. Add drained spinach; cook, stirring, for 2 more minutes. Leave to cool slightly. Stir in coriander, nutmeg and cheese. Add beaten egg and mix well. Season. In a small pan, melt butter. Brush one sheet of pastry with butter. Lay it in cake tin, pressing well down into corners. Leave pastry hanging over edge of tin.

Brush a second sheet of pastry with butter and lay it in tin at right angles to first sheet. Repeat with remaining pastry. Spoon spinach mixture into tin. Fold excess pastry over filling to cover it. Leave pastry in slight folds to look untidy. Brush with melted butter. Bake in oven for 40 minutes until golden brown and crisp. Cut into 9 squares. Serve hot, warm or cold, garnished with coriander leaves.

Makes 9.

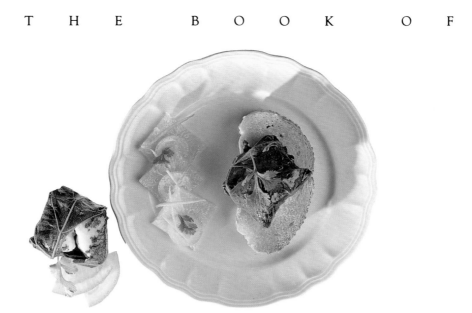

— VINE LEAF-WRAPPED CHEESE —

8 vacuum-packed vine leaves
225 g (8 oz) haloumi cheese
2 teaspoons chopped fresh coriander
salt and pepper
2 teaspoons olive oil
TO SERVE:
8 thick slices long thin Greek bread
1 clove garlic

Select 8 small vine leaves from the vacuum pack. The rest may be frozen for use another time.

Rinse vine leaves thoroughly in several changes of cold water. Pat dry. Cut cheese into 8 cubes. Toss cheese in chopped coriander, then season with salt and pepper. Wrap each piece of cheese in a vine leaf. Brush with oil. Heat grill and grill cheese parcels for a few minutes, turning once or twice until cheese heats through.

Toast bread on both sides. Cut the garlic clove in half and rub the toasted bread with the cut surfaces. Serve the toast with the grilled cheese parcels.

Serves 8.

——————— IMAM BAYALDI ———————

2 small aubergines (eggplants)
salt
55 ml (2 fl oz / ¼ cup) olive oil
1 large onion, chopped
1 clove garlic, crushed
1 red pepper (capsicum), seeded and chopped
6 teaspoons tomato purée (paste)
55 g (2 oz) sun-dried tomatoes in oil, drained and
    chopped
½ teaspoon sugar
1 teaspoon wine vinegar
pepper
toasted pine nuts and coriander sprigs, to garnish

Cut aubergines (eggplants) into 0.5 cm
(¼ in) slices. Sprinkle with salt and put in a
colander to drain for 30 minutes. Preheat
oven to 180C (350F/Gas 4). In a frying pan,
heat 2 tablespoons olive oil, add onion, garlic
and red pepper (capsicum). Cook for about
10 minutes until onion is soft. Add tomato
purée (paste), sun-dried tomatoes, sugar,
vinegar and pepper.

Wipe aubergine (eggplant) slices dry with
absorbent kitchen paper. Arrange slices in a
baking tin. Put a teaspoonful of tomato
mixture onto each aubergine (eggplant)
slice. Drizzle remaining olive oil over and
around aubergines (eggplants). Cover dish
and bake for 40-50 minutes until aubergines
(eggplants) are tender. Serve garnished with
toasted pine nuts and sprigs of coriander.

Serves 6.

AUBERGINE SALAD

2 aubergines (eggplants)
1 clove garlic, crushed
6 teaspoons mayonnaise
6 teaspoons yogurt
salt and pepper
2 tablespoons chopped fresh parsley
pitta bread and sticks of raw vegetables, to serve

Bring a saucepan of water to the boil. Add aubergines (eggplants) to pan and cook for 30 minutes or until quite soft.

Drain aubergines (eggplants). As soon as they are cool enough to handle, cut them down the middle and scrape the flesh away from the skins with a teaspoon. Leave to cool. Put aubergine (eggplant) flesh, garlic, mayonnaise and yogurt in a food processor and process until smooth. Season to taste with salt and pepper.

Transfer aubergine (eggplant) purée to a serving bowl. Chill for 1 hour. Garnish with parsley and serve with pitta bread and sticks of raw vegetables.

Serves 6.

———— COURGETTE SALAD ————

2 tablespoons pine nuts
450 g (1 lb) courgettes (zucchini)
2 tablespoons olive oil
1 clove garlic, crushed
2 tablespoons currants
2 teaspoons chopped fresh mint
juice ½ lemon
salt and pepper
2 spring onions

Put pine nuts in a large frying pan and cook, stirring, until just beginning to brown. Remove pine nuts and reserve. Top and tail courgettes (zucchini) and slice thinly.

Heat oil in frying pan, add courgettes (zucchini), garlic, currants and pine nuts. Cook, stirring, until courgettes (zucchini) are just beginning to soften and brown slightly.

Stir in mint, lemon juice, salt and pepper. Transfer to a serving dish and leave until cold. Slice the spring onions and scatter them over the top.

Serves 4.

—— FRIED HALOUMI SALAD ——

a selection of salad leaves
225 g (8 oz) haloumi cheese
1 egg, beaten
55 g (2 oz/1 cup) breadcrumbs
oil for frying
marigold petals, to garnish
SALAD DRESSING:
70 ml (2½ fl oz/⅓ cup) olive oil
3 teaspoons balsamic vinegar
1 teaspoon lemon juice
1 teaspoon Dijon mustard
salt and pepper

Wash and dry salad leaves. Arrange on 6 individual plates.

To make dressing, in a screw-top jar, mix together oil, vinegar, lemon juice, mustard, salt and pepper. Screw on lid and shake vigorously. Cut cheese into 1 cm (½ in) cubes. Put beaten egg in a bowl and bread-crumbs on a board or plate. Toss cheese in egg, then in breadcrumbs.

Heat oil in a deep frying pan. Fry cheese until golden brown. Drain on absorbent paper. Pour the dressing over the salad. Arrange cubes of cheese on each plate. Scatter with marigold petals and serve immediately.

Serves 6.

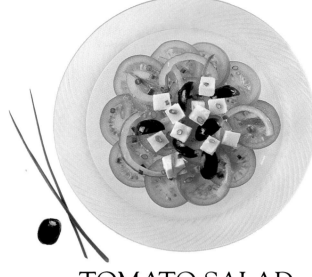

──────── TOMATO SALAD ────────

225 g (8 oz) small tomatoes
½ small red onion
10-12 black olives
DRESSING:
4 tablespoons olive oil
1 tablespoon lemon juice
1 teaspoon chopped fresh mint
2 teaspoons chopped fresh chives
1 teaspoon clear honey
salt and pepper

To make dressing, in a bowl, mix together olive oil, lemon juice, mint, chives, honey and salt and pepper.

Cut tomatoes into slices. Slice onion thinly. Place in a serving bowl with olives.

Stir dressing and pour over tomatoes. Toss together to coat tomatoes with dressing. Serve with Greek bread.

Serves 4.

Variation: Cubes of feta cheese may be added to this salad.

GARLIC PEPPER SALAD

1 small green pepper (capsicum)
1 small red pepper (capsicum)
1 small yellow pepper (capsicum)
1 small purple pepper (capsicum)
2 cloves garlic, finely chopped
115 ml (4 fl oz/½ cup) olive oil
3 teaspoons lemon juice
3 teaspoons balsamic vinegar
salt and pepper
chopped fresh parsley, fresh basil leaves and
     nasturtium flowers, to garnish (optional)

Cut all the peppers (capsicums) into quarters.
Remove seeds and core.

Preheat grill. Grill peppers (capsicums), skin
side up, until black and blistered. Put in a
plastic bag and leave for 10 minutes; then
scrape off the blistered skin. Slice peppers
(capsicums) lengthways in strips.

Arrange on a serving dish in groups of alternating coloured strips. Scatter with chopped
garlic. In a bowl, whisk together oil, lemon
juice, vinegar, salt and pepper, then pour
mixture over the peppers (capsicums). Leave
to marinate for 2-3 hours. Serve garnished
with chopped parsley, basil leaves and nasturtium flowers, if available.

Serves 6.

MARINATED OLIVES

115 g (4 oz) green olives
2 thin lemon slices
2 teaspoons coriander seeds
2 cloves garlic
olive oil to cover
115 g (4 oz) black olives
¼ red pepper (capsicum)
1 small hot chilli
1 sprig thyme

Place green olives in a jar. Cut each lemon slice into quarters and add to olives. Lightly crush coriander seeds and 1 clove garlic and add to the green olives. Cover with olive oil and seal jar.

Place black olives in a separate jar. Crush remaining garlic and cut pepper (capsicum) and chilli into strips, removing seeds. Add to olives with sprig of thyme. Cover with olive oil and seal jar.

Leave in marinade for at least 2 days before transferring to a serving bowl and serving with other mezes. If the jars are resealed the olives will keep indefinitely. The oil can be used for salad dressings and cooking.

Serves 6.

BEAN DIP

6 teaspoons olive oil
1 onion, finely chopped
225 g (8 oz) dried butter beans, soaked overnight, then drained
juice ½ lemon
1 teaspoon sugar
salt and pepper
1 teaspoon paprika
3 teaspoons chopped fresh dill
2 red peppers (capsicums)
paprika, olive oil and sprigs of dill, to garnish
pitta bread and sticks of raw vegetables, to serve

In a saucepan, heat 3 teaspoons oil. Add onion and cook gently until soft. Add 450 ml (16 fl oz/2 cups) water and beans. Bring to the boil. Boil for 10 minutes; then reduce heat and simmer, covered, for 1½ hours until very soft. Add more water if necessary. Drain beans, reserving the water. In a food processor, process beans, remaining oil, lemon juice, sugar, salt, pepper, paprika and chopped dill, adding enough cooking water to make a smooth purée. Cover closely with plastic wrap and leave to cool.

Cut red peppers (capsicums) in half and scoop out seeds. Stand pepper (capsicum) halves on a flat plate and fill with bean purée. Garnish with a sprinkling of paprika, a drizzle of olive oil and a sprig of dill. Serve with pitta bread and sticks of raw vegetables.

Serves 4.

TZATZIKI

1 cucumber
2½ teaspoons salt
1 clove garlic
1 tablespoon chopped fresh mint
200 g (7 oz) Greek sheeps' milk yogurt
pepper
mint leaves, to garnish
pitta bread, to serve

Peel cucumber and cut into small dice. Place in a colander, sprinkle with 2 teaspoons salt and leave to drain for 1 hour.

Pat cucumber dry with absorbent paper. Crush garlic with remaining salt until creamy.

In a bowl, mix together garlic, chopped mint and yogurt. Season with pepper. Stir in diced cucumber. Transfer to a serving bowl. Garnish with mint leaves and serve at once with pitta bread.

Serves 6.

——— STUFFED TOMATOES ———

85 g (3 oz/½ cup) long-grain rice
4 large or 8 medium tomatoes
4 spring onions, chopped
2 cloves garlic, crushed
2 teaspoons chopped fresh mint
salt and pepper
4 teaspoons olive oil
toasted pine nuts, to garnish (optional)

Cook rice in a saucepan of boiling salted water for 7-8 minutes or until barely cooked. Drain and rinse.

Preheat oven to 180C (350F/Gas 4). Cut a thin slice off the top of each tomato. Carefully scoop out the flesh and place it in a sieve to drain. Chop half the flesh (the remainder can be saved for sauces or soup). Put chopped flesh in a bowl with rice, spring onions, garlic, mint, salt and pepper.

Place tomatoes in an ovenproof dish and fill them with stuffing. Drizzle a little olive oil over each tomato. Cover dish and bake in the oven for 25-30 minutes (less for small tomatoes) until soft but not losing their shape. Garnish with toasted pine nuts, if desired.

Serves 4 or 8.

── CORIANDER MUSHROOMS ──

225 g (8 oz) small button mushrooms
1 teaspoon coriander seeds
9 teaspoons olive oil
1 teaspoon lemon juice
9 tablespoons dry white wine
1 clove garlic, crushed
1 sprig thyme
salt and pepper
4 tablespoons chopped fresh parsley, to garnish

Wipe mushrooms with a damp cloth and trim stalks. Crush coriander seeds in a mortar and pestle.

In a frying pan, heat oil. Add coriander seeds and heat them for a few seconds. Add lemon juice, white wine, garlic, thyme, salt and pepper and bring to the boil. Add mushrooms to pan, stir well, cover and simmer for 10 minutes.

With a slotted spoon, transfer mushrooms to a serving dish. Boil liquid for a minute or two to reduce a little, then pour it over the mushrooms. Leave to cool completely. Scatter chopped parsley over the top before serving.

Serves 4.

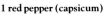

——— GRILLED VEGETABLES ———

1 red pepper (capsicum)
2 baby courgettes (zucchini)
2 baby aubergines (eggplants)
1 fennel bulb
8 baby sweetcorn
salt and pepper
courgette flowers and basil sprigs, to garnish
MARINADE:
150 ml (5 fl oz/⅔ cup) olive oil
2 cloves garlic, crushed
1 teaspoon chopped fresh parsley
1 teaspoon chopped fresh mint
1 teaspoon chopped fresh oregano

To make marinade, in a bowl mix together olive oil, garlic, parsley, mint and oregano. Cut red pepper (capsicum) into quarters, lengthways. Remove seeds and core. Cut courgettes (zucchini) in half lengthways. Cut aubergines (eggplants) in half lengthways. Cut fennel bulb into quarters. Put pepper (capsicum), courgettes (zucchini), aubergines (eggplants), fennel and sweetcorn into the bowl with the marinade. Leave for at least 1 hour.

Preheat grill or barbecue. Grill vegetables for about 10 minutes, or until tender. Turn them every few minutes and brush with marinade. Season with salt and pepper. Garnish with courgette flowers and basil sprigs.

Serves 4.

Variation: A wide variety of vegetables can be grilled. Try mushrooms, tomatoes, chicory, onions and squashes.

LEEKS À LA GRECQUE

8-10 young thin leeks
9 teaspoons olive oil
6 teaspoons lemon juice
1 clove garlic, crushed
salt and pepper
1 tablespoon chopped fresh mint
slivers of sun-dried tomatoes and mint leaves, to
garnish

Cut root end off leeks and trim tops down to white part. Wash very carefully.

In a saucepan, put olive oil, lemon juice, 115 ml (4 fl oz/½ cup) water, garlic, salt and pepper. Bring to the boil. Add leeks, cover and cook for 10-15 minutes until leeks are tender.

Transfer leeks to a serving dish. If there is a lot of liquid, boil to reduce and thicken slightly, then pour it over the leeks. Scatter chopped mint over the top and leave until cold. Serve garnished with slivers of sun-dried tomatoes and mint leaves.

Serves 4-8.

Variation: Button onions may be cooked in the same way.

AUBERGINE FRITTERS

2 small aubergines (eggplants)
salt
oil for frying
2 lemons, cut into quarters
BATTER:
115 g (4 oz/1 cup) plain flour
pinch salt
25 g (1 oz/6 teaspoons) butter, melted
1 egg white

To make batter, sift flour and salt into a large
bowl. Add melted butter and 175 ml (6 fl oz/
¾ cup) tepid water, beating to form a smooth
thick cream. Leave to stand for 1 hour.

Slice aubergines (eggplants) into 0.5 cm (¼
in) slices. Place in a colander, sprinkle with
salt and leave to drain for 30 minutes. In a
bowl, whisk egg white until stiff. Fold into
batter. Pat aubergine (eggplant) slices dry
with absorbent kitchen paper.

In a frying pan, heat 1 cm (½ in) oil. Dip
aubergine (eggplant) slices into batter. Fry in
batches for 2 minutes, then turn over and fry
for a further 2 minutes until crisp and golden
on both sides. Keep warm while frying
remaining slices. Drain on absorbent paper.
Serve at once, with lemon quarters.

Serves 6.

— STUFFED COURGETTE RINGS —

85 g (3 oz) bulgar wheat
6 courgettes (zucchini) about 15 cm (6 in) long
3 teaspoons olive oil
1 small onion, finely chopped
2 teaspoons tomato purée (paste)
1 teaspoon chopped fresh mint
salt and pepper
6 teaspoons lemon juice
fresh vine leaves, to serve
fresh herbs, to garnish

Put bulgar wheat in a bowl. Pour in enough boiling water to come well above the wheat. Leave to soak for 1 hour. Drain thoroughly.

Preheat oven to 180C (350F/Gas 4). Cut rounded ends off courgettes (zucchini). With a small apple corer, carefully remove centres from courgettes (zucchini). In a frying pan, heat oil. Cook onion until soft. Remove from heat. Stir in bulgar wheat, tomato purée (paste), mint, salt and pepper. Press stuffing firmly into the hollowed-out courgettes (zucchini).

Place courgettes (zucchini) in an ovenproof dish. Pour over lemon juice and 4 table-spoons water. Cover dish and bake in the oven for 45 minutes or until courgettes (zucchini) are cooked but still firm enough to slice neatly. With a sharp knife, cut cour-gettes (zucchini) into 3 mm (⅛ in) slices. Serve on a plate lined with vine leaves, garnished with fresh herbs.

Serves 6.

DOLMADES

20 vacuum-packed vine leaves in brine
85 g (3 oz/½ cup) long-grain rice
salt and pepper
2 tablespoons olive oil
1 small onion, finely chopped
55 g (2 oz/⅓ cup) pine nuts
25 g (1 oz/¼ cup) raisins
2 tablespoons chopped fresh mint
¼ teaspoon ground cinnamon
2 teaspoons olive oil
6 teaspoons tomato purée (paste)
2 teaspoons lemon juice
lemon slices and fresh mint, to garnish (optional)

Rinse vine leaves and place in a saucepan of boiling water. Simmer for 5 minutes. Drain. Put rice into a pan of boiling salted water, cover and simmer until rice is almost cooked. Drain. In a frying pan, heat oil, then add onion and cook until soft. Add pine nuts and cook until lightly browned. Stir in raisins, mint, cinnamon, salt, pepper and rice. Leave to cool.

Trim stalks from vine leaves. Place a little filling on each leaf. Fold sides over and roll up. Line a saucepan with any damaged leaves. Place dolmades side by side in pan, to fit tightly. In a bowl, mix 300 ml (10 fl oz/ 1¼ cups) water, 2 teaspoons olive oil, tomato purée (paste) and lemon juice. Pour over dolmades. Place a plate on top. Cover pan and simmer for 1-1½ hours until liquid is absorbed and leaves are tender. Garnish with lemon and mint, if desired, and serve hot.

Makes 20.

TARAMASALATA

115 g (4 oz) smoked cod's roe
3 slices white bread, crusts removed
2 cloves garlic, crushed
juice 1 lemon
85 ml (3 fl oz/⅓ cup) olive oil
4 tablespoons yogurt
½ teaspoon paprika
½ small onion, grated
30-40 cherry tomatoes and slivered black olives, to
    serve

Scrape cod's roe from skin and put in a
blender or food processor.

Soak bread in a little water then crumble into
blender or processor. Process until smooth.
With the motor running, add garlic, lemon
juice, olive oil, yogurt and paprika. Add
more lemon juice or olive oil if necessary for
flavour or consistency. Finally add onion.

Cut tops off tomatoes and carefully scoop out
flesh and seeds. Leave upside down on absorbent kitchen paper for 30 minutes. Spoon
taramasalata into tomatoes. Top each one
with a sliver of black olive.

Serves 6.

FRIED SQUID

700 g (1½ lb) small squid
seasoned flour
oil for deep frying
BATTER:
115 g (4 oz / 1 cup) plain flour
pinch salt
25 g (1 oz / 6 teaspoons) butter, melted
1 egg white
GREEN MAYONNAISE:
1 bunch watercress, washed and trimmed
300 ml (10 fl oz / 1¼ cups) mayonnaise

To make batter, sift flour and salt into a large bowl. Add melted butter, then gradually add 175 ml (6 fl oz / ¾ cup) tepid water, beating continuously to form a smooth thick cream. Leave to stand for 1 hour. To make mayonnaise, in a food processor, purée watercress with 1 tablespoon boiling water. In a bowl, mix watercress purée and mayonnaise. Set aside.

Clean squid. Pull on tentacles; cut off just above head, discarding head and innards. Slip quill-like bone out of body. Rinse body, pulling away outer skin. Dry on absorbent kitchen paper. Cut body and tentacles into rings. In a bowl, whisk egg white. Fold into batter. Heat oil in a deep fryer. Dip squid into seasoned flour, then into batter. Fry a few pieces at a time, until brown and crisp. Drain. Serve with mayonnaise.

Serves 6.

SEAFOOD PARCELS

85 g (3 oz / ²⁄₃ cup) butter
25 g (1 oz / ¼ cup) flour
150 ml (5 fl oz / ²⁄₃ cup) milk
6 teaspoons lemon juice
1 clove garlic, crushed
1 tablespoon each chopped fresh mint, chopped fresh
　coriander and chopped fresh parsley
pinch cayenne pepper
pinch paprika
½ teaspoon ground cumin
salt
85 g (3 oz) cooked mussels
55 g (2 oz) cooked peeled prawns
55 g (2 oz) cooked squid or white fish
6 sheets filo pastry

Preheat oven to 190C (375F/Gas 5). In a saucepan, melt 25 g (1 oz/6 teaspoons) butter. Stir in flour, then gradually add milk. Stirring, heat sauce until thick. Stir in lemon juice, garlic, mint, coriander, parsley, cayenne, paprika, cumin and salt. Add mussels, prawns and squid or white fish.

Melt remaining butter. Brush over 1 sheet filo pastry, place another sheet on top and butter it. Repeat with 2 more layers of pastry. Cut into 12 squares. Butter remaining 2 sheets of pastry. Place one on top of the other. Cut in half. Pile the 4 sheets together; cut into 6 squares. Place some filling in middle of each square. Draw pastry up and pinch together to form pouches. Bake for 30 minutes or until brown and crisp.

Makes 18.

GRILLED MUSSELS

20 mussels
½ onion, chopped
1 bouquet garni
1 clove garlic, finely chopped
3 teaspoons chopped fresh fennel
3 teaspoons chopped fresh oregano
salt and pepper
25 g (1 oz/½ cup) breadcrumbs
115 ml (4 fl oz/½ cup) olive oil
fennel sprigs, to garnish

Scrub mussels and remove beards. Discard any which do not close when tapped. Put into a saucepan with 300 ml (10 fl oz/1¼ cups) water, onion and bouquet garni.

Cover, bring to the boil and cook for 1-2 minutes, shaking pan occasionally, until mussels have opened. Strain. Remove top half of each shell. In a bowl, mix together garlic, fennel, oregano, salt, pepper and breadcrumbs.

Preheat grill. Arrange mussels in an oven-proof dish. Sprinkle with breadcrumb mixture. Pour 1 teaspoon of olive oil over each mussel. Place mussels under grill until heated through and browned. Serve garnished with fennel sprigs.

Serves 4.

SWORDFISH KEBABS

juice ½ lemon
12 teaspoons olive oil
1 tablespoon chopped fresh fennel
1 tablespoon chopped fresh chives
1 clove garlic, crushed
salt and pepper
450 g (1 lb) swordfish
1 small onion
16 cherry tomatoes
lemon slices and fresh herbs, to garnish

In a bowl, mix together lemon juice, olive oil, fennel, chives, garlic, salt and pepper. Cut swordfish into 2 cm (¾ in) cubes. Place in bowl of marinade and leave for 1 hour. Cut onion into quarters and separate layers.

Preheat grill. Thread swordfish, onion and tomatoes onto 8 skewers. Grill for 5-10 minutes, turning frequently and brushing with any remaining marinade. Serve garnished with lemon slices and herb sprigs.

Serves 8.

MEATBALLS IN TOMATO SAUCE

1 slice bread, crusts removed
450 g (1 lb) minced lamb
1 clove garlic, crushed
1 onion, finely chopped
1 tablespoon chopped fresh parsley
1 tablespoon chopped fresh mint
½ teaspoon ground cinnamon
salt and pepper
flour for rolling
6 teaspoons olive oil
fresh herbs, to garnish
TOMATO SAUCE:
3 teaspoons olive oil
1 small onion, chopped
400 g (14 oz) can chopped tomatoes
1 teaspoon sugar

Soften bread in a little water. Squeeze dry, then crumble into a mixing bowl. Add lamb, garlic, finely chopped onion, parsley, mint, cinnamon, salt and pepper to bowl and mix thoroughly. On a floured board, roll meat mixture into small balls.

To make the sauce, heat oil in a saucepan. Add onion and cook until soft. Add tomatoes, salt, pepper and sugar. Cook gently for 5 minutes. In a blender or food processor, process sauce until smooth. Return to pan and reheat. In a frying pan, heat oil and fry meatballs for 5-6 minutes, turning frequently, until browned and cooked through. Transfer to a warmed serving dish and pour sauce over the top. Garnish and serve.

Serves 6.

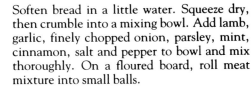

——— MINCED MEAT FINGERS ———

3 teaspoons pine nuts
55 ml (2 fl oz/¼ cup) olive oil
1 onion, finely chopped
350 g (12 oz) lean minced beef
1 teaspoon ground cinnamon
1 tablespoon chopped fresh parsley
salt and pepper
6 sheets filo pastry
1 quantity Tzatziki, see page 25, to serve

In a frying pan, heat pine nuts until golden. Remove from pan and set aside.

Heat 6 teaspoons oil in frying pan, add onion and cook until soft. Stir in beef and cook, stirring, for a few minutes until brown all over. Add cinnamon, parsley, pine nuts, salt and pepper. Cook for a further 10 minutes, then leave to cool.

Preheat oven to 180C (350F/Gas 4). Cut each sheet of filo pastry into 3 long strips. Brush strips with remaining oil. Spread 1 teaspoon of filling in a line on one end of each strip, leaving a small margin on either side. Roll over twice and fold long sides over the edge, then continue rolling to make a tube. Place fingers on a baking sheet. Bake in the oven for 20-30 minutes until crisp and golden. Serve with Tzatziki.

Makes 18.

KEFTEDES

2 slices bread, crusts removed
350 g (12 oz) minced steak
1 tablespoon chopped fresh dill
½ teaspoon ground cumin
1 small egg, beaten
1 teaspoon ouzo
salt and pepper
flour for dusting
3 tablespoons olive oil
fennel sprigs and lemon wedges, to garnish
SAUCE:
150 ml (5 fl oz/⅔ cup) yogurt
1 tablespoon chopped fresh coriander

Soak bread in a little water. Squeeze dry and crumble into a bowl.

Add minced steak, dill, cumin, egg, ouzo, salt and pepper. Mix thoroughly. Spread meat mixture onto a plate. Divide into 16 equal segments. Roll each segment into a ball, then flatten to form a patty. Put some flour on a plate; dip each patty into flour.

To make the sauce, in a bowl, mix together yogurt and coriander and season with salt and pepper. In a frying pan, heat oil. Fry keftedes for 3-4 minutes on each side until well browned and cooked through. Garnish with fennel sprigs and lemon wedges and serve with the yogurt sauce.

Makes 16.

PORK KEBABS

450 g (1 lb) lean pork
1 onion
1 green pepper (capsicum)
8 cherry tomatoes
shredded lettuce, orange slices and thyme sprigs, to
    garnish
MARINADE:
juice ½ orange
2 tablespoons olive oil
1 clove garlic, crushed
1 teaspoon chopped fresh thyme
1 teaspoon coriander seeds, crushed
salt and pepper

To make the marinade, in a bowl, mix together orange juice, olive oil, garlic, thyme, coriander seeds, salt and pepper. Cut pork into 2 cm (¾ in) cubes and add to marinade. Mix thoroughly, cover and leave in a cool place for 2 hours. Cut onion into quarters and separate the layers. Cut pepper (capsicum) into small squares, removing seeds.

Thread pork, onion, pepper (capsicum) and tomatoes onto 8 bamboo satay skewers. Grill on a barbecue or under a grill, turning from time to time, for 10-15 minutes until pork is cooked through. Serve on a bed of shredded lettuce, garnished with orange slices and thyme.

Makes 8.

SOUVLAKIA

2 cloves garlic, crushed
55 ml (2 fl oz/¼ cup) lemon juice
2 tablespoons olive oil
4 tablespoons chopped fresh oregano
salt and pepper
450 g (1 lb) lean lamb
6 bay leaves
oregano sprigs, to garnish
RED PEPPER SAUCE:
3 teaspoons olive oil
1 small onion, chopped
2 red peppers (capsicums), seeded and chopped
225 ml (8 fl oz/1 cup) chicken stock

In a bowl, mix together garlic, lemon juice, olive oil, oregano, salt and pepper. Cut lamb into 2 cm (¾ in) cubes. Put lamb into marinade. Mix well to coat lamb with marinade. Leave in a cool place for 2 hours. To make the sauce, in a saucepan, heat oil, add onion and cook until soft. Add red peppers (capsicums); cook over low heat for 5 minutes. Pour in stock and simmer for 10 minutes. Push through a sieve or purée in a blender or food processor.

Thread lamb onto skewers, placing bay leaves on skewers at intervals. Grill on a barbecue or under a hot grill, turning from time to time, for 10 minutes or until lamb is brown and crisp on the outside and pink and juicy inside. Garnish with oregano and serve with the sauce.

Serves 6.

—CUCUMBER & YOGURT SOUP—

1 large cucumber
550 ml (20 fl oz/2 ½ cups) yogurt
2 teaspoons lemon juice
6 teaspoons chopped fresh mint
salt and pepper
300 ml (10 fl oz/1 ¼ cups) chilled milk
chopped chives, to garnish

Rinse cucumber and trim ends; do not peel.
Grate cucumber quite finely, into a bowl.

Stir in yogurt, lemon juice and mint. Season
well with salt and pepper. Cover bowl and
chill for 2 hours.

Stir in the chilled milk. Pour soup into 6
individual bowls. Scatter chopped chives
over soup and serve.

Serves 6.

AVGOLEMONO SOUP

1 litre (35 fl oz/4½ cups) well-flavoured chicken stock
salt and pepper
25 g (1 oz/2 tablespoons) long-grain rice
2 eggs
55 ml (2 fl oz/¼ cup) lemon juice
6 lemon slices and tarragon sprigs, to garnish

In a saucepan, heat chicken stock. Season with salt and pepper. Bring to the boil. Add rice to chicken stock. Cover pan and simmer for 10-15 minutes until rice is cooked.

In a bowl, beat together eggs and lemon juice. Strain into another bowl. Add a ladleful of hot stock to egg mixture. Whisk and pour back into pan.

Heat gently, stirring, for 3-4 minutes until soup thickens. Do not allow to boil. Pour into 6 warmed soup bowls. Serve garnished with a slice of lemon and a sprig of tarragon.

Serves 6.

Note: The best chicken stock for this recipe is made from the liquid saved from boiling a chicken.

FISHERMAN'S SOUP

fish trimmings
2 onions, sliced
70 ml (2½ fl oz/⅓ cup) olive oil
2 bay leaves
2 sprigs parsley
1 small sprig thyme
4 tomatoes, peeled and roughly chopped
8 peppercorns
salt
1 kg (2.2 lb) fish such as mullet, snapper, bream or
    John Dory, skinned and filleted
8 large Mediterranean (king) prawns, preferably raw
16 mussels, cleaned, (see page 36)
2-3 teaspoons lemon juice
narrow French loaf
chopped fresh parsley, to garnish

In a large saucepan, put fish trimmings, onions, olive oil, bay leaves, parsley, thyme, tomatoes, peppercorns and salt. Add 2 litres (2¼ pints/9 cups) water and bring to the boil. Simmer gently, uncovered, for 45 minutes. Press through a sieve into a clean pan.

Cut fish into 2.5 cm (1 in) cubes. Bring stock to simmering point. Add fish and prawns, if raw. Simmer for 5 minutes, or until fish is nearly cooked. It must not overcook, or it will disintegrate. Finally, add mussels and cooked prawns, if using. Cook for 1-2 minutes until mussels open. Add lemon juice to taste. Meanwhile, make croûtons. Cut the French loaf into slices. Bake in a medium oven until dry and crisp. Garnish the soup with parsley and serve with the croûtons.

Serves 8.

BEAN SOUP

450 g (1 lb) dried haricot beans
1 leek
1 onion
2 carrots
3 stalks celery, with leaves
55 ml (2 fl oz/¼ cup) olive oil
2 cloves garlic, crushed
6 teaspoons tomato purée (paste)
salt and pepper
chopped fresh parsley and chopped black olives, to
    garnish

Put beans in a bowl. Pour over boiling water
to cover. Leave for 1 hour.

Drain the beans, rinse, then put in a large
saucepan. Add 2.5 litres (4¼ pints/11¼
cups) water, bring to the boil and simmer for
30 minutes. Meanwhile, slice leek, onion,
carrots and celery. In a saucepan, heat oil.
Add leek, onion, carrots, celery and garlic.
Stir to coat vegetables with oil; cover pan and
cook gently for 5 minutes.

When beans have cooked for 30 minutes, add
vegetables and tomato purée (paste), then
cover and cook for a further 1-1½ hours until
beans are tender and beginning to split.
Season with salt and pepper. Add more water
if desired. Serve garnished with chopped
parsley and olives.

Serves 6-8.

——— LENTIL & TOMATO SOUP ———

2 tablespoons olive oil
1 large onion, chopped
2 cloves garlic, chopped
3 stalks celery, chopped
400 g (14 oz) can chopped tomatoes
225 g (8 oz/1¼ cups) brown lentils
2 tablespoons chopped fresh parsley
1 bay leaf
salt and pepper
1 tablespoon lemon juice
yogurt and 1 tablespoon each chopped fresh basil and
     mint, to garnish

In a large saucepan, heat oil. Add onion and garlic and cook until soft. Add celery, tomatoes, lentils, parsley and bay leaf to pan. Stir in 2 litres (3½ pints/9 cups) water and bring to the boil. Cover pan and simmer for 1¾ hours until soup is thick and lentils and vegetables are very soft.

In a blender or food processor, purée soup until smooth. Return to saucepan. Soup should be thick, but add more water if a thinner consistency is preferred. Season well. Add lemon juice. Serve soup in warmed bowls with a spoonful of yogurt floating in centre and herbs scattered over.

Serves 6-8.

Variation: This soup may be served without being puréed, if preferred.

-CUCUMBER & TOMATO SALAD-

4 tomatoes
½ cucumber
1 bunch spring onions
1 bunch purslane or watercress, washed
1 teaspoon chopped fresh mint
1 teaspoon chopped fresh fennel
70 ml (2½ fl oz/⅓ cup) olive oil
6 teaspoons lemon juice
salt and pepper
halved stuffed olives, to garnish

Put tomatoes in a bowl. Pour boiling water over. Leave for 1 minute, then put into cold water. Leave for 1 minute, peel, cut into small dice and put in a bowl.

Peel cucumber, cut into small dice and add to tomatoes. Trim and chop spring onions and add to tomato and cucumber.

Break the purslane or watercress into small sprigs. Mix with tomato and cucumber. In a bowl, whisk together mint, fennel, olive oil, lemon juice, salt and pepper. Pour over salad. Serve garnished with halved stuffed olives.

Serves 4.

SQUID SALAD

450 g (1 lb) small squid
55 ml (2 fl oz/¼ cup) olive oil
1 small red onion, finely chopped
6 teaspoons dry white wine
1 clove garlic, crushed
salt and pepper
3 teaspoons lemon juice
1 tablespoon chopped fresh parsley
lemon rind strips and parsley sprigs, to garnish

Clean squid. Pull on tentacles; cut off just above head, discarding head and innards. Slip quill like transparent bone out of body.

Rinse body inside and out, pulling away pink outer membrane. Dry on absorbent paper. Cut body into 0.5 cm (¼ in) rings and cut tentacles into small pieces. Heat 6 teaspoons olive oil in a frying pan. Add onion; cook until it softens and just begins to colour. Add squid; fry gently for 5 minutes, stirring. Add wine and garlic. Cook, covered, for 5-10 minutes until squid is tender.

Leave to cool in pan. Transfer squid and onion to a serving dish. Add remaining oil, salt, pepper, lemon juice and parsley to pan. Stir, then spoon it over the squid. Serve garnished with lemon rind and parsley sprigs.

Serves 4.

THREE BEAN SALAD

85 g (3 oz) dried flageolet beans
85 g (3 oz) dried red kidney beans
2 sprigs thyme
450 g (1 lb) fresh broad beans, podded
1 small onion, finely chopped
red pepper (capsicum) rings, to garnish
DRESSING:
115 ml (4 fl oz/½ cup) olive oil
juice 1 lemon
1 tablespoon chopped fresh mint
1 tablespoon chopped fresh parsley
salt and pepper

Put the flageolet and the kidney beans in 2 separate bowls.

Cover with water to come well above top of beans. Leave to soak for at least 6 hours. Drain. Put flageolet and kidney beans in 2 separate saucepans each with a sprig of thyme. Cover with water. Bring to the boil and boil briskly for 10 minutes. Cover pans and simmer for 1-1½ hours until beans are tender. In a pan of boiling water, cook broad beans for 5-10 minutes until tender. Drain all the beans and put into a bowl.

To make the dressing, in a bowl, mix together oil, lemon juice, mint, parsley, salt and pepper. Pour dressing over warm beans. Add chopped onion and mix well. Leave until cold, then transfer to a serving dish. Serve the salad garnished with rings of red pepper (capsicum).

Serves 6.

COUNTRY SALAD

2 Little Gem lettuces
6 tomatoes
½ cucumber
1 bunch spring onions
2 tablespoons chopped fresh mint
2 teaspoons chopped fresh oregano
55 ml (2 fl oz/¼ cup) olive oil
6 teaspoons lemon juice
salt and pepper
175 g (6 oz) feta cheese
12 black olives

Wash and dry lettuces. Roll up the leaves and slice across to make shreds. Scatter them over a serving dish.

Cut tomatoes into quarters and arrange on lettuce. Score down side of cucumber with a fork or knife to make grooves, then slice cucumber and arrange on lettuce. Chop spring onions and scatter then over the salad with mint and oregano.

In a bowl, mix together oil, lemon juice, salt and pepper. Pour over salad. Cut feta cheese into cubes and arrange on the salad with olives. Serve immediately.

Serves 6.

MANGE TOUT SALAD

450 g (1 lb) mange tout (snow peas)
55 ml (2 fl oz/¼ cup) olive oil
juice ½ lemon
salt and pepper
1 clove garlic
1 tablespoon chopped fresh coriander
1 tablespoon chopped fresh mint
lemon rind strips, to garnish

Top and tail mange tout (snow peas). In a large saucepan, heat 1 tablespoon oil, add mange tout (snow peas) and stir to coat with oil.

Add enough water to cover mange tout (snow peas). Bring to the boil, cover and cook for about 5 minutes until mange tout (snow peas) are just cooked and still have a slight crunch. Drain and return to pan.

Pour lemon juice and remaining oil over mange tout (snow peas). Add salt and pepper and mix well. Turn into a serving dish and leave to cool. Before serving, chop garlic finely and scatter over mange tout (snow peas) with coriander and mint; garnish with lemon rind.

Serves 4-6.

LENTIL SALAD

225 g (8 oz/1 ¼ cups) green lentils
55 ml (2 fl oz/¼ cup) olive oil
1 onion, finely chopped
3 tomatoes, peeled and chopped
salt and pepper
1 tablespoon chopped fresh parsley
2 tablespoons lemon juice
onion rings, chopped fresh parsley and lemon slices, to
   garnish

Put lentils in a bowl, cover with cold water and leave to soak for 3-4 hours. Drain well.

In a large saucepan, heat half the oil, add onion and cook until soft. Add tomatoes, cook for 1 minute, then add lentils. Cover with water, cover pan and simmer gently for 30 minutes, adding water if necessary, until lentils are tender and all water has been absorbed. The lentils should still be holding their shape.

Add salt, pepper, parsley, lemon juice and remaining oil to lentils. Mix carefully, then transfer to a serving dish and leave to cool. Serve garnished with onion rings, chopped parsley and lemon slices.

Serves 4-6.

— GREEN BEANS WITH ONION —

450 g (1 lb) green beans
9 teaspoons olive oil
2 onions, chopped
1 clove garlic, crushed
4 teaspoons tomato purée (paste)
1 tablespoon chopped fresh oregano
salt and pepper
finely chopped red pepper (capsicum) or oregano sprig,
  to garnish

Top and tail beans. In a large saucepan, heat oil. Add onions and garlic. Cook for 5-10 minutes until soft.

Mix the tomato purée (paste) with 175 ml (6 fl oz/¾ cup) water. Put beans in pan with onion. Pour tomato mixture over them, then add more water, if necessary, to just cover the beans.

Add oregano, salt and pepper. Cover pan and simmer for 15-20 minutes until beans are tender. Remove lid and boil to reduce the liquid. Serve garnished with chopped red pepper (capsicum) or a sprig of oregano.

Serves 4.

– BROAD BEANS & ARTICHOKES –

700 g (1 ½ lb) broad beans, shelled
400 g (14 oz) can artichoke hearts
3 teaspoons olive oil
1 teaspoon cornflour
3 teaspoons lemon juice
1 tablespoon chopped fresh parsley
salt and pepper
chopped fresh parsley, to garnish

In a saucepan of boiling water, cook beans for 10 minutes or until tender. Drain, reserving 55 ml (2 fl oz/¼ cup) of the water.

Drain and rinse artichoke hearts; cut in half. In a saucepan, heat olive oil. Add broad beans and artichokes. In a bowl, mix cornflour and lemon juice and stir into reserved cooking water. Stir parsley, salt and pepper into cornflour mixture.

Pour cornflour mixture over beans and artichokes. Bring to the boil and cook until sauce is slightly thickened. Serve with more parsley scattered over the top.

Serves 6.

—— BROAD BEANS WITH DILL ——

1 kg (2.2 lb) fresh broad beans
55 ml (2 fl oz/¼ cup) olive oil
1 onion, finely chopped
1 clove garlic, crushed
2 tablespoons chopped fresh dill
salt and pepper
dill sprigs, to garnish
yogurt, to serve

Shell broad beans. In a saucepan, heat oil. Add onion and garlic and cook gently until just beginning to colour.

Add beans and cook gently for 2-3 minutes. Add enough hot water to just cover beans, stir in chopped dill and season with salt and pepper. Cook, covered, for 10 minutes or until beans are tender.

When beans are tender, remove lid and cook briskly until liquid has almost evaporated. Garnish with sprigs of dill and serve with yogurt.

Serves 6.

BEANS & GREENS

225 g (8 oz) dried beans
1 clove garlic
bouquet garni of thyme, parsley and oregano
450 g (1 lb) chard or young cabbage leaves, shredded
salt and pepper
6 teaspoons olive oil
3 teaspoons lemon juice
lemon slices, to garnish

Put beans in a bowl, cover with cold water and leave to soak for about 6 hours. Drain well.

Put beans in a saucepan. Pour in enough cold water to come 5 cm (2 in) above beans. Add garlic and bouquet garni. Bring to the boil and boil briskly for 10 minutes. Cover pan and cook for a further 1-1½ hours until beans are tender.

Add shredded chard or cabbage and simmer gently for 5 minutes until cabbage is tender. Drain thoroughly. Return to pan; stir in salt, pepper, olive oil and lemon juice. Serve garnished with lemon slices.

Serves 4-6.

Note: This dish may also be served cold, if preferred.

─BLACK-EYED BEANS & RICE─

225 g (8 oz) dried black-eyed beans
3 teaspoons lemon juice
6 teaspoons olive oil
1 large onion, finely chopped
1 clove garlic, crushed
85 g (3 oz/½ cup) long-grain rice, rinsed and drained
salt and pepper
2 teaspoons white wine vinegar
chopped fresh herbs and green olives, to garnish

Wash and drain beans, place in a saucepan; cover with cold water. Bring to the boil and boil for 2 minutes.

Drain, discarding water. Return beans to pan; cover with fresh water to come well above surface of beans. Add lemon juice. Bring to boil; cover and boil for 20-30 minutes until beans are tender.

In another saucepan, heat oil, add onion and garlic and cook until soft. Add rice, stir to coat with oil, then add 175 ml (6 fl oz/¾ cup) water and season with salt. Bring to the boil; cover pan and simmer for 10-15 minutes until rice is tender and water absorbed. Drain beans and mix with rice. Add vinegar, salt and pepper. Heat together for 2 minutes. Serve garnished with chopped herbs and olives.

Serves 4-6.

FASOULIA

55 ml (2 fl oz/¼ cup) olive oil
1 clove garlic, crushed
3 large tomatoes, skinned and chopped
225 g (8 oz) dried haricot beans, soaked overnight
1 bay leaf
1 sprig thyme
salt and pepper
onion rings and thyme sprigs, to garnish

In a large saucepan, heat oil. Add garlic and tomatoes. Cook for a few minutes until tomatoes soften.

Drain beans and add to pan. Pour in boiling water to come 2.5 cm (1 in) above top of beans. Add bay leaf and thyme. Cover pan and simmer for 1-1¼ hours until beans are tender.

The liquid should have reduced to form a thick sauce. If not, simmer uncovered for a few minutes. Season with salt and pepper. Transfer beans to a serving dish. Serve garnished with onion rings and sprigs of thyme.

Serves 4.

POURGOURI PILAFF

1 onion
2 tomatoes
1 small green pepper (capsicum)
6 teaspoons olive oil
25 g (1 oz) cut vermicelli
225 g (8 oz) bulgar wheat
350 ml (12 fl oz/1 ½ cups) chicken stock
salt and pepper
coriander sprigs, to garnish

Slice onion thinly. Put tomatoes in a bowl; pour boiling water over. Leave for 1 minute.

Transfer tomatoes to a bowl of cold water. Leave for another minute. Drain and peel off skins. Cut tomatoes in half, then slice. Quarter pepper (capsicum) and remove core and seeds, then slice. In a large saucepan, heat oil, add onion and pepper (capsicum) and cook until onion is soft. Add vermicelli and stir to coat with oil.

Put bulgar wheat in a colander and rinse in cold water, then add to pan. Stir in chicken stock and bring to the boil. Cover pan and simmer for 5 minutes. Add tomatoes and simmer for a further 5-10 minutes until bulgar wheat is tender and stock is absorbed. Add more water if necessary. Stir in salt and pepper. Transfer to a serving dish and garnish with coriander.

Serves 6.

POTATO KEPHTEDES

450 g (1 lb) potatoes
2 tomatoes, peeled
3 teaspoons olive oil
salt and pepper
1 tablespoon chopped fresh parsley
4 spring onions, finely chopped
55 g (2 oz/½ cup) plain flour, sifted
flour for dusting
oil for frying
rings of green part of spring onion and dill sprigs, to
    garnish

Peel the potatoes and cut them into evenly
sized pieces.

Put in a pan of water, bring to the boil and
cook, covered, for 20 minutes until tender.
Drain and leave to cool. Cut tomatoes into
quarters, remove seeds and chop flesh. Add
tomatoes, olive oil, salt, pepper, parsley,
chopped spring onions and flour to potatoes.
Mix thoroughly.

Knead mixture lightly. On a floured board
roll out to a thickness of 1 cm (½ in). Cut out
8 rounds. Heat oil in a frying pan. Fry potato
cakes for 6-7 minutes, turning once, until
golden and crisp. Serve at once, garnished
with rings of spring onion and sprigs of dill.

Serves 8.

SPINACH & RICE

450 g (1 lb) spinach
1 bunch spring onions
55 ml (2 fl oz/¼ cup) olive oil
1 tablespoon chopped fresh dill
115 g (4 oz/¾ cup) long-grain rice
salt and pepper
dill sprigs and chopped tomato, to garnish

Trim stalks from spinach, wash leaves well. In a saucepan, put spinach and just the water that clings to leaves. Boil for 5 minutes.

Drain spinach thoroughly and leave to cool, then squeeze dry and chop. Cut spring onions (including some of green part) into thin slices. In a saucepan, heat oil, add spring onions and cook until soft. Add spinach and dill. Cook gently for a further 5 minutes.

Put rice in a sieve and rinse under running water. Drain and then add to spinach. Stir rice until coated with oil. Add 300 ml (10 fl oz/1¼ cups) hot water. Bring to the boil; cover pan and simmer for 15-20 minutes until rice is cooked and water is absorbed. Add salt and pepper. Press rice into 6 ramekins or tea cups. Turn out onto warmed plates. Serve garnished with dill and chopped tomato.

Serves 6.

— COURGETTES WITH CHEESE —

700 g (1 ½ lb) courgettes (zucchini)
6 teaspoons olive oil
1 large onion, chopped
1 teaspoon chopped fresh mint
2 eggs
175 g (6 oz/1 ½ cups) grated kefalotiri cheese
¼ teaspoon freshly grated nutmeg
salt and pepper

Preheat oven to 180C (350F/Gas 4). Trim courgettes (zucchini) ends, then cut into 1 cm (½ in) slices. Put courgette (zucchini) slices into a steamer above boiling water. Cook in batches, if necessary. Steam for a few minutes until just tender.

In a frying pan, heat oil, add onion and cook until soft. Mix courgettes (zucchini) and mint with the softened onion, then put in an ovenproof dish.

In a bowl, beat eggs with cheese, nutmeg, salt and pepper, then pour over the courgettes (zucchini). Bake in the oven for 20 minutes or until top is lightly browned.

Serves 4.

Variation: This dish may also be made with marrow instead of courgettes.

OKRA & TOMATOES

450 g (1 lb) small okra
55 ml (2 fl oz/¼ cup) olive oil
1 small onion, chopped
1 small leek, chopped
450 g (1 lb) tomatoes, peeled and chopped
1 clove garlic, crushed
3 teaspoons lemon juice
salt and pepper
1 teaspoon sugar
chopped fresh parsley, to garnish

Cut stalks off okra. Wash pods, drain; pat dry. Do not pierce pods.

In a large shallow pan, heat oil, add onion and leek and cook slowly until softened and lightly coloured. Add okra and turn carefully in the oil. Cook for 5 minutes.

Add tomatoes, garlic, lemon juice, salt, pepper and sugar. Cover pan and simmer gently for 10 minutes. Remove lid and cook for a further 10 minutes or until okra is tender and sauce reduced to a small quantity. If sauce reduces too quickly, add a little water. Garnish with chopped parsley and serve.

Serves 6.

FISH PLAKI

6 teaspoons olive oil
2 onions, sliced
2 cloves garlic, crushed
4 large tomatoes, peeled and chopped
juice ½ lemon
2 tablespoons chopped fresh parsley
1 bay leaf
1 teaspoon dried oregano
salt and pepper
1 kg (2.2 lb) bream
chopped green olives, to garnish

In a saucepan, heat oil. Add onions and garlic and cook gently for 5-10 minutes until onions are soft.

Stir in tomatoes, lemon juice, parsley, bay leaf, oregano, salt and pepper. Cover and simmer gently for 10 minutes. Meanwhile, preheat oven to 200C (400F/Gas 6).

Place fish in a baking dish and pour over the sauce. Bake in the oven for 20-30 minutes until flesh is cooked and flakes easily when tested with a fork. Scatter chopped olives over fish and serve at once.

Serves 4.

FISH FRITTERS WITH SKORDALIA

1 kg (2.2 lb) fish fillets, such as cod or John Dory
flour seasoned with salt and pepper
oil for deep frying
BATTER:
115 g (4 oz/1 cup) plain flour
1 teaspoon chopped fresh parsley
25 g (1 oz/6 teaspoons) butter, melted
1 egg white
SKORDALIA:
3 cloves garlic, crushed
5 cm (2 in) thick slice white bread
115 g (4 oz/1 ¼ cups) ground almonds
115 ml (4 fl oz/½ cup) olive oil
2 teaspoons lemon juice

Make the batter. Sift flour and a pinch of salt into a large bowl. Stir in parsley. Add melted butter and gradually add 175 ml (6 fl oz/ ¾ cup) tepid water, beating to form a smooth thick cream. Leave to stand for 1 hour. Meanwhile, make the skordalia. Put garlic in a blender or food processor. Remove crusts from bread. Squeeze bread in a little cold water, then add to garlic with ground almonds and a little olive oil.

With the motor running, gradually add remaining oil. Stir in lemon juice and salt and pepper to taste. In a bowl, whisk egg white, then fold into batter mixture. Heat oil in a deep fryer or pan. Cut fish into 6 pieces. Dip in seasoned flour then in batter. Fry for 8-10 minutes according to thickness of fish. Drain on absorbent paper, then serve with the skordalia.

Serves 6.

— PRAWNS & SAFFRON SAUCE —

juice ½ lemon
3 tablespoons olive oil
2 cloves garlic, crushed
3 teaspoons chopped fresh fennel
salt and pepper
16 raw Mediterranean (king) prawns
lemon slices and fennel sprigs, to garnish (optional)
SAFFRON SAUCE:
150 ml (5 fl oz/⅔ cup) fish stock
4 saffron threads
150 ml (5 fl oz/⅔ cup) mayonnaise
1 teaspoon lemon juice

In a bowl, mix together lemon juice, oil, garlic, fennel, salt and pepper.

Put prawns in a dish and pour the marinade over them. Leave in a cool place for 2 hours. To make the saffron sauce, in a saucepan, boil fish stock until reduced to 3 teaspoons. Add saffron threads. Leave to cool. Strain stock into a bowl and stir in the mayonnaise. Add salt, pepper and lemon juice.

Preheat grill. Thread prawns onto skewers and grill for 10 minutes, turning once. Remove from skewers. Garnish with lemon slices and fennel, if desired, and serve with saffron sauce.

Serves 4.

PRAWN & FETA TARTS

175 g (6 oz) peeled cooked prawns
115 g (4 oz) feta cheese
fresh basil leaves, to garnish
PASTRY:
175 g (6 oz/1 ½ cups) plain flour
½ teaspoon salt
9 teaspoons olive oil
1 egg, beaten
TOMATO SAUCE:
6 teaspoons olive oil
1 onion, chopped
1 clove garlic, crushed
200 g (7 oz) can chopped tomatoes
3 teaspoons chopped sun-dried tomato
2 teaspoons chopped fresh basil
salt and pepper

To make the pastry, sift flour and ½ teaspoon salt into a bowl. With a fork, mix in olive oil, egg and 1-2 teaspoons water to make a firm dough. Knead lightly, wrap in plastic wrap and chill for 1 hour. Make tomato sauce. Heat oil in a frying pan, add onion and garlic; cook until soft. Add tomatoes and sun-dried tomato. Cook for 5-10 minutes until sauce is very thick. Stir in basil, salt and pepper. Preheat oven to 200C (400F/Gas 6).

On a floured surface, roll out pastry thinly. Line four 10 cm (4 in) loose-bottom flan tins with pastry and press a piece of foil into each. Bake in the oven for 10 minutes. Remove foil; cook for a further 5 minutes. Divide prawns between pastry cases. Crumble cheese over. Spread tomato sauce over cheese and prawns. Bake for 5 minutes. Serve garnished with basil leaves.

Serves 4.

—— SQUID & PRAWN KEBABS ——

350 g (12 oz) cleaned squid, see page 34
juice ½ lemon
2 teaspoons clear honey
6 teaspoons olive oil
8 large raw peeled prawns
salt and pepper
lemon slices and chopped fresh parsley, to garnish
GARLIC MAYONNAISE:
4 cloves garlic
2 egg yolks
300 ml (10 fl oz/1 ¼ cups) olive oil
juice ½ lemon

Cut squid into 0.5 cm (¼ in) rings. In a bowl, mix together lemon juice, honey and 6 teaspoons oil. Add squid. Cover and leave in a cool place for 6 hours. To make the mayonnaise, crush garlic to a smooth pulp using a pestle and mortar. Put garlic in a blender or food processor with egg yolks and a little salt. With the motor running, gradually pour in half the olive oil. When mixture begins to thicken, add lemon juice and pepper. Add remaining oil.

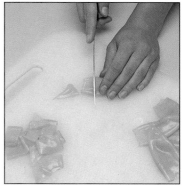

Drain squid and pat dry with absorbent kitchen paper. Thread onto wooden skewers, alternating with prawns. Season with salt and pepper. Grill for 4-5 minutes, turning constantly, until golden. Cut lemon slices in half and dip cut edges in chopped parsley. Garnish kebabs with the lemon slices and serve with garlic mayonnaise.

Serves 4 as a starter.

GRILLED SARDINES

1 kg (2.2 lb) fresh sardines, cleaned and scaled
6 teaspoons coarse sea salt
1 tablespoon chopped fresh oregano
1 tablespoon chopped fresh parsley
1 tablespoon chopped fresh fennel
lemon slices, to garnish
AVGOLEMONO SAUCE:
400 ml (14 fl oz/1¾ cups) fish stock
salt and pepper
3 teaspoons cornflour
2 large egg yolks
juice 1 lemon

Slash each sardine twice on each side. Sprinkle with sea salt; put herbs inside cavities. Leave for 30 minutes. To make the sauce, put fish stock in a saucepan, season and heat. In a bowl, mix cornflour with a little water. Whisk hot stock into cornflour mixture. Return to pan. Cook gently for 10-15 minutes, stirring, until sauce thickens. In a bowl, beat egg yolks. Stir in lemon juice. Add a little of hot sauce; return sauce to pan. Cook gently, without boiling, until thickened.

Preheat grill. Grill sardines for 1½-2 minutes on each side until skins are brown and crisp. Garnish the fish with lemon slices and serve with the sauce.

Serves 4.

——SQUID WITH RED WINE——

700 g (1½ lb) squid
55 ml (2 fl oz/¼ cup) olive oil
1 large onion, chopped
2 cloves garlic, crushed
450 g (1 lb) tomatoes, peeled and roughly chopped
150 ml (5 fl oz/⅔ cup) red wine
salt and pepper
½ teaspoon sugar
2.5 cm (1 in) cinnamon stick
3 teaspoons chopped fresh parsley
6 slices bread, crusts removed, and 9 teaspoons olive
    oil, to serve

Clean squid, see page 34. Cut into rings. Dry
thoroughly with absorbent paper. In a large
saucepan, heat oil. Add onion and garlic and
cook until soft. Add squid and fry until lightly
browned. Add tomatoes, wine, salt, pepper,
sugar and cinnamon. Simmer, uncovered, for
30 minutes or until squid is tender. Stir in
parsley.

Sauce should be thick and rich. If not, transfer squid to a hot dish and boil sauce to
reduce. Cut bread into triangles. In a frying
pan, heat oil and fry bread until golden on
both sides. Serve squid in individual dishes,
with fried bread tucked round the sides.

Serves 6.

BAKED GREY MULLET

6 teaspoons olive oil
2 red onions, thinly sliced
1 clove garlic, crushed
1 kg (2.2 lb) grey mullet, cleaned
1 sprig fennel
1 sprig parsley
salt and pepper
115 ml (4 fl oz/½ cup) dry white wine
55 g (2 oz/1 cup) breadcrumbs
fennel sprigs, to garnish

Preheat the oven to 180C (350F/Gas 4). In a frying pan, heat oil. Add onions and cook gently for 10 minutes until soft.

Put garlic in the cavity of the fish with sprigs of fennel and parsley. Season fish with salt and pepper, inside and out.

Spread softened onions over base of a baking dish. Place fish on onions and pour the wine over. Sprinkle with breadcrumbs. Cover dish and bake in the oven for 10 minutes, then uncover dish and cook for a further 10-15 minutes until flesh flakes away from the bones when tested with a knife. Serve garnished with sprigs of fennel.

Serves 4.

Variation: 4 small mullet could be used instead of 1 large one.

───── STUFFED AUBERGINES ─────

3 aubergines (eggplants)
salt and pepper
2 teaspoons olive oil
1 onion, finely chopped
450 g (1 lb) minced lamb or beef
2 tomatoes, skinned and chopped
3 teaspoons tomato purée (paste)
3 teaspoons chopped fresh oregano
1/2 teaspoon ground cinnamon
55 ml (2 fl oz/1/4 cup) dry white wine
CHEESE SAUCE:
25 g (1 oz/6 teaspoons) butter
25 g (1 oz/1/4 cup) flour
300 ml (10 fl oz/1 1/4 cups) milk
85 g (3 oz/3/4 cup) grated kefalotiri cheese

Cut aubergines (eggplants) lengthways, from stalk, sprinkle with salt and leave to drain for 1 hour. In a saucepan, heat oil. Add onion and cook until soft. Add lamb and stir until brown. Add tomatoes, tomato purée (paste), oregano, cinnamon, salt, pepper, wine and 55 ml (2 fl oz/1/4 cup) water. Cover and cook gently for 15 minutes. Remove lid and cook until mixture is dry. Dry aubergines (eggplants). Scoop out pulp. Chop half and mix with meat mixture (reserve other half for another dish).

Preheat oven to 180C (350F/Gas 4). To make the sauce, in a saucepan, melt butter. Stir in flour; cook for 2 minutes, stirring, over gentle heat. Remove from heat. Gradually stir in milk. Return to heat. Stir until thick and smooth. Cook gently for 5 minutes. Season. Stir in two thirds of cheese. Fill each aubergine (eggplant) shell two thirds full of meat mixture. Top with cheese sauce. Sprinkle with remaining cheese. Bake for 20 minutes until brown.

Serves 6.

MOUSSAKA

700 g (1½ lb) aubergines (eggplants)
salt and pepper
olive oil
2 onions, finely chopped
700 g (1½ lb) minced lamb or beef
2 tomatoes, peeled and chopped
6 teaspoons tomato purée (paste)
3 teaspoons chopped fresh oregano
1 teaspoon ground cinnamon
115 ml (4 fl oz/½ cup) dry white wine
WHITE SAUCE:
55 g (2 oz/¼ cup) butter
55 g (2 oz/½ cup) plain flour
450 ml (16 fl oz/2 cups) milk
150 ml (5 fl oz/⅔ cup) yogurt
25 g (1 oz/¼ cup) grated kefalotiri cheese

Thinly slice aubergines and put in a colander. Sprinkle with salt and leave to drain for 1 hour. In a saucepan, heat 3 teaspoons oil. Add onions and cook until soft. Add lamb and stir until brown. Add tomatoes, tomato purée (paste), oregano, cinnamon, salt, pepper, wine and 115 ml (4 fl oz/½ cup) water. Cover; cook gently for 30 minutes. Remove lid; cook until mixture is dry. Dry aubergines. Heat 2.5 cm (½ in) oil in a frying pan. Fry aubergines, turning once, until beginning to brown. Drain on absorbent paper. Preheat oven to 180C (350F/Gas 4).

To make sauce, melt butter; stir in flour and cook for 2 minutes over a gentle heat. Remove from heat. Gradually stir in milk and yogurt. Return to heat. Stir until thick and smooth. Cook gently for 5 minutes. Season. Put a layer of aubergine (eggplant) in an ovenproof dish. Cover with half meat then half remaining slices. Cover with remaining mince and aubergine (eggplant) slices. Pour sauce over top. Sprinkle with cheese. Bake for 40 minutes until brown.

Serves 6.

— LAMB STEAKS WITH PASTA —

4 thick lamb leg steaks
salt and pepper
2 cloves garlic, sliced
400 g (14 oz) can chopped tomatoes
70 ml (2½ fl oz/⅓ cup) olive oil
3 teaspoons chopped fresh marjoram
3 teaspoons chopped fresh parsley
315 g (10 oz) orzo (rice-shaped pasta)
salad leaves, to serve

Preheat oven to 200C (400F/Gas 6). Season meat with salt and pepper. Place in a large roasting tin.

Scatter garlic over meat. Add 150 ml (5 fl oz/⅔ cup) water and tomatoes. Stir in olive oil, salt, pepper, marjoram and parsley. Cook for 40 minutes, basting from time to time and turning pieces of lamb over.

Add 300 ml (10 fl oz/1¼ cups) boiling water and the pasta. Stir in more salt and pepper. Cook for a further 40 minutes until pasta is cooked. If necessary, add more hot water. Serve with salad leaves.

Serves 6.

LAMB PARCELS

12 vine leaves, preserved in brine
55 ml (2 fl oz/¼ cup) olive oil
juice ½ lemon
2 cloves garlic, crushed
3 teaspoons chopped fresh marjoram
salt and pepper
6 sheets filo pastry
55 g (2 oz/¼ cup) butter, melted
6 thin lamb steaks or pieces of lamb fillet
shredded nasturtium flowers and mint, to garnish

Soak vine leaves in water for 1 hour. In a saucepan of boiling water, cook vine leaves for 5 minutes. Drain and dry on a tea towel.

In a bowl, mix together olive oil, lemon juice, garlic, marjoram, salt and pepper. Place lamb in a dish, pour marinade over and leave in a cool place for 1 hour.

Preheat oven to 190C (375F/Gas 5). Brush each sheet of filo pastry with butter. Lay a vine leaf in middle of one end of each sheet. Place a lamb steak on top, then cover with another vine leaf. Fold sides of pastry over lamb and roll up to form neat parcels. Place on a baking sheet. Bake in the oven for 20-30 minutes until pastry is golden and crisp. Serve garnished with shredded nasturtium flowers and mint.

Serves 6.

BAKED LAMB WITH VEGETABLES

1 leg of lamb, weighing about 2.25 kg (4½ lb)
3 cloves garlic, cut into slivers
salt and pepper
1 aubergine (eggplant)
700 g (1½ lb) potatoes, peeled
1 large onion, thinly sliced
450 (1 lb) tomatoes, sliced
55 ml (2 fl oz/¼ cup) white wine
1 tablespoon chopped fresh oregano

Preheat oven to 220C (425F/Gas 7). Cut slits
in meat and insert slivers of garlic. Rub
generously with salt and pepper. Place lamb
in a large roasting tin and put in oven.

Reduce heat to 180C (350F/Gas 4) and roast
for 1½ hours for slightly pink meat or 2 hours
for medium-well done. Meanwhile, slice
aubergine (eggplant) into 0.5 cm (¼ in)
slices, place in a colander and sprinkle with
salt. Leave for 30 minutes, then rinse and pat
dry with absorbent kitchen paper.

One hour before the end of cooking time
remove any fat from roasting tin and add
vegetables. Pour the wine over, season with
salt and pepper and sprinkle with oregano.
Return to the oven. Turn vegetables over
during the cooking time to cook them evenly
in juices. Carve lamb into slices, adding any
meat juices to vegetables. Serve lamb with
the vegetables and meat juices.

Serves 6.

SPICED RACK OF LAMB

3 teaspoons plain flour
salt and pepper
2 racks of lamb
1 clove garlic, finely chopped
6 teaspoons olive oil
450 g (1 lb) tomatoes, roughly chopped
½ lemon, chopped
1 stick cinnamon
3 cloves
1 small red chilli, seeded and chopped
115 ml (4 fl oz/½ cup) dry white wine
6 teaspoons tomato purée (paste)
lemon slices, to garnish

Preheat oven to 180C (350F/Gas 4). Mix together flour, salt and pepper. Rub over lamb. Press garlic into gaps between bones. In a roasting tin, heat oil. Put lamb, skin side down, in oil to brown. Remove lamb. Add tomatoes, lemon, cinnamon, cloves and chilli to roasting tin. Return lamb, skin side up, to tin.

In a bowl, mix together wine, 115 ml (4 fl oz/½ cup) water and tomato purée (paste). Pour over lamb. Cover tin loosely with foil. Cook in the oven for 1 hour. Remove foil and cook for a further 30 minutes until lamb is cooked. Cut lamb into individual chops and keep warm. Place roasting tin on heat and boil liquid to reduce to a thick sauce. Pour over meat. Garnish with lemon slices.

Serves 6.

PORK WITH PEARS

6 teaspoons olive oil
2 onions, chopped
1 kg (2.2 lb) boned lean pork, cut into cubes
250 ml (9 fl oz/1 cup) red wine
grated rind ½ orange
½ cinnamon stick
salt and pepper
2 pears
2 teaspoons clear honey
chopped fresh coriander leaves, orange rind strips and
    pitta bread, to garnish

In a flameproof casserole, heat oil. Add onions; cook until soft. Push to side of pan, turn up heat and brown meat in batches.

Add wine, orange rind, cinnamon stick, salt, pepper and 300 ml (10 fl oz/1¼ cups) water. Bring to simmering point, then cover casserole and cook for 1 hour.

Peel, core and slice pears and place on top of meat. Drizzle honey over pears. Cover pan and simmer gently for 30-40 minutes until meat is tender. Garnish with chopped coriander leaves, strips of orange rind and pieces of pitta bread.

Serves 6.

Note: This recipe is traditionally made with quinces. If quinces are available, use them instead of pears.

AFELIA

625 g (1¼ lb) pork fillet
1 teaspoon coriander seeds
1 teaspoon soft brown sugar
salt and pepper
3 teaspoons olive oil
250 ml (9 fl oz/1 cup) red wine
fresh coriander leaves, to garnish

Cut pork into 1 cm (½ in) slices. Place slices between 2 sheets greaseproof paper and beat with a rolling pin to flatten slightly.

In a mortar and pestle, lightly crush coriander seeds with the sugar and salt and pepper to taste. Sprinkle the crushed mixture onto both sides of the pork. Leave in a cool place for at least 30 minutes.

In a frying pan, heat oil. Add pork in batches and brown on both sides. Return pork to pan. Pour in the wine, allow to bubble up for a minute, then reduce heat and cook, un-covered, for 20-30 minutes until pork is tender. The liquid should have reduced to a syrupy consistency. If not, transfer pork to a serving dish and keep hot. Boil liquid until reduced; pour it over the meat and garnish with coriander leaves.

Serves 4.

SPICY BRAISED BEEF

1.35 kg (3 lb) beef topside joint
2 cloves garlic, crushed
½ teaspoon ground cinnamon
¼ teaspoon ground cloves
salt and pepper
9 teaspoons olive oil
4 onions, thinly sliced
115 ml (4 fl oz/½ cup) red wine
6 teaspoons tomato purée (paste)
450 g (1 lb) spaghetti
3 teaspoons balsamic vinegar
fresh herbs, to garnish

With a sharp knife, make slits in the beef.

In a bowl, mix garlic, cinnamon, cloves, salt and pepper, press mixture into slits and leave beef in a cool place for 1 hour. Heat oil in a flameproof casserole into which meat will just fit. Turn meat in hot oil until brown all over. Remove from casserole. Add onions and cook gently until soft and lightly browned. Replace meat. Add the wine and enough hot water to barely cover it. Mix tomato purée (paste) with a little water; stir into casserole. Season.

Cover casserole and cook over a gentle heat for about 1½ hours, turning meat frequently, until it is tender. Bring a large pan of salted water to the boil and cook spaghetti until *al dente*. Remove meat and keep hot. Add vinegar to sauce. Boil briskly until reduced to a smooth glossy sauce. Slice beef. Garnish with herbs and serve with some sauce poured over beef and remainder stirred into spaghetti.

Serves 6.

PASTITSIO

225 g (8 oz) macaroni
6 teaspoons olive oil
1 onion, chopped
1 clove garlic, crushed
450 g (1 lb) minced steak
300 ml (10 fl oz/1 ¼ cups) stock
2 teaspoons tomato purée (paste)
½ teaspoon ground cinnamon
1 teaspoon chopped fresh mint
salt and pepper
55 g (2 oz/¼ cup) butter
55 g (2 oz/½ cup) plain flour
450 ml (16 fl oz/2 cups) milk
115 ml (4 fl oz/½ cup) yogurt
175 g (6 oz/1 ½ cups) grated kefalotiri cheese

In a pan of boiling water, cook macaroni for 8 minutes until tender. Drain, rinse with cold water and set aside. Preheat oven to 190C (375F/Gas 5). In a frying pan, heat oil, add onion and garlic and cook until soft. Add mince and stir until browned. Stir in stock, tomato purée (paste), cinnamon, mint, salt and pepper. Cook gently for 10-15 minutes until sauce is reduced.

In a saucepan, melt butter. Stir in flour; cook for 1 minute. Gradually stir in milk and yogurt; cook gently for 5 minutes. Stir in half cheese. Season. Mix macaroni into cheese sauce. Spread half macaroni mixture over base of a large gratin or soufflé dish. Cover with meat sauce; top with remaining macaroni. Sprinkle remaining cheese over top. Bake for 45 minutes until browned.

Serves 4-6.

SOFRITO

55 ml (2 fl oz/¼ cup) olive oil
1 onion, finely chopped
1 clove garlic, crushed
700 g (1½ lb) thin veal slices
seasoned flour
6 teaspoons brandy
150 ml (5 fl oz/⅔ cup) white wine
300 ml (10 fl oz/1¼ cups) beef stock
salt and pepper
3 tablespoons chopped fresh parsley
parsley, to garnish

In a frying pan, heat oil. Add onion and garlic; cook until soft. Transfer to a flame-proof casserole.

Coat meat lightly with seasoned flour. Fry in frying pan until brown on both sides. Add brandy. When brandy has stopped bubbling, transfer meat to casserole.

Add wine, stock, salt and pepper. Cover and cook gently for 45 minutes until meat is tender and sauce lightly thickened. Stir in parsley. Garnish with more parsley.

Serves 6.

- VEAL CHOPS WITH TOMATOES -

6 teaspoons olive oil
4 veal chops or steaks
1 large onion, sliced
1 clove garlic, crushed
200 g (7 oz) can chopped tomatoes
1 teaspoon tomato purée (paste)
salt and pepper
1 teaspoon dried oregano
½ teaspoon ground cinnamon
toasted pine nuts and oregano sprigs, to garnish

In a frying pan, heat olive oil. Add chops. Cook on one side until sealed; turn and brown other side. Transfer to a plate and keep warm.

Add onion and garlic to pan and cook for a few minutes until soft. Stir in tomatoes, tomato purée (paste), salt, pepper, oregano, cinnamon and 150 ml (5 fl oz/⅔ cup) water.

Return chops to pan. Spoon some of the sauce over them. Simmer gently, uncovered, for 20 minutes or until chops are cooked and sauce is thick. Scatter toasted pine nuts and sprigs of oregano over the top before serving.

Serves 4.

—————— LEMON CHICKEN ——————

55 g (2 oz/¼ cup) butter
grated rind and juice 1 lemon
3 teaspoons chopped fresh oregano
1.8 kg (4 lb) chicken
115 ml (4 fl oz/½ cup) chicken stock
salt and pepper
lemon slices and parsley sprigs, to garnish
SAUCE:
3 eggs
juice ½ lemon

Preheat oven to 180C (350F/Gas 4). Place half butter, the lemon rind and most of oregano inside chicken.

Heat remaining butter in a large flameproof casserole, put in chicken and brown all over. Pour in lemon juice, stock, salt, pepper and remaining oregano. Cover casserole and cook in the oven for 1¼-1½ hours until chicken is cooked and juices run clear when the thickest part is pierced. Transfer chicken to a heated dish. Measure 250 ml (9 fl oz/1 cup) of the cooking liquid.

To make the sauce, in a bowl, whisk together eggs and lemon juice. Gradually whisk in hot cooking liquid. Place bowl over a pan of simmering water and heat gently, stirring, until sauce is thick and smooth. Add salt and pepper. Carve chicken and arrange on a hot serving plate. Pour the sauce over the chicken. Garnish with slices of lemon and parsley sprigs.

Serves 6.

GRILLED CHICKEN

55 ml (2 fl oz/¼ cup) olive oil
juice ½ lemon
3 teaspoons chopped fresh marjoram
3 teaspoons chopped fresh thyme
6 chicken breasts
cooked rice, to serve
salt and pepper
thyme and marjoram sprigs and lemon rind strips,
    to garnish

In a shallow dish, mix together oil, lemon juice, marjoram and thyme.

Prick chicken flesh with a fork. Turn chicken pieces in marinade, then cover the dish and leave in a cool place for up to 8 hours.

Preheat grill. Remove chicken from marinade and place, skin side down, under grill. Brush with marinade mixture and grill for 8-10 minutes, basting occasionally with marinade. Turn chicken pieces over and grill for a further 8-10 minutes until golden brown and cooked through. Stir pan juices into rice and season. Serve chicken with the rice, garnished with sprigs thyme and marjoram and strips of lemon rind.

Serves 6.

KLEFTIKO

1 chicken, weighing 1.35 kg (3 lb)
1 lemon, quartered
2 teaspoons dried oregano
salt and pepper
6 teaspoons olive oil
1 red onion, finely sliced
115 ml (4 fl oz/½ cup) dry white wine
lemon rind strips and oregano sprigs, to garnish

Preheat oven to 170C (325F/Gas 3). Cut chicken into 4 portions. Rub each chicken portion all over with a lemon quarter.

Mix together dried oregano, 1 teaspoon salt and pepper to taste. Rub mixture over each chicken portion. Cut 4 squares of foil large enough to wrap around a chicken portion. Brush foil with olive oil. Place a piece of chicken in the middle of each foil square. Scatter sliced onion over chicken. Pour 5-6 teaspoons wine over each piece of chicken.

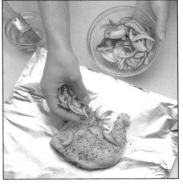

Seal edges of foil to make a parcel. Place parcels on a baking sheet and bake in the oven for 1-1½ hours until chicken is well cooked and the juices run clear when the thickest part is pierced with a knife. To serve, open each parcel and slide contents onto a warmed plate. Garnish with lemon rind and sprigs of oregano.

Serves 4.

CHICKEN PIE

1.5 kg (3¼-3½ lb) chicken
chicken stock
450 g (1 lb) onions, sliced
150 ml (5 fl oz/⅔ cup) milk
115 g (4 oz/½ cup) butter, melted
3 teaspoons lemon juice
115 g (4 oz/1 cup) grated kefalotiri cheese
salt and pepper
¼ teaspoon freshly grated nutmeg
3 teaspoons chopped fresh parsley
2 eggs, beaten
12 sheets filo pastry
salad leaves, to garnish

Put chicken in a flameproof casserole into which it fits tightly. Pour in enough stock to almost cover legs. Cover chicken breast with a sheet of buttered greaseproof paper. Cover casserole and simmer for 1 hour or until chicken is just cooked. Remove chicken from casserole and leave to cool.

Add onions and milk to stock. Boil rapidly uncovered, until liquid is reduced to 300 ml (10 fl oz/1¼ cups) of thick pulpy onion sauce. Preheat oven to 180C (350F/Gas 4).

Remove skin from chicken. Cut meat into neat pieces and place in a large bowl. Add onion sauce, half the butter, the lemon juice, cheese, salt, pepper, nutmeg, parsley and eggs. Mix well together.

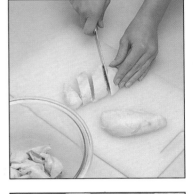

Lightly butter a 20 x 30 cm (8 x 12 in) roasting tin. Brush one sheet of pastry with butter and place in tin, overlapping edges. Brush 5 more sheets of pastry and layer them on top.

Spread the filling over the pastry. Flap over-lapping pastry over top. Cut remaining sheets of pastry to fit tin. Brush with butter and layer on top. Score top into squares and sprinkle with water. Bake for 45 minutes or until golden brown and crisp. Serve with salad leaves.

Serves 6-8.

ROAST STUFFED POUSSIN

2 poussins weighing about 800 g (1¾ lb) each
30 g (1 oz/6 teaspoons) butter for spreading
salt and pepper
STUFFING:
25 g (1 oz) dried chestnuts
55 g (2 oz/¼ cup) rice
25 g (1 oz/¼ cup) shelled pistachio nuts
25 g (1 oz/¼ cup) currants
salt and pepper
½ teaspoon ground cinnamon
55 g (2 oz/¼ cup) butter

Make the stuffing. Put chestnuts in a bowl; cover with cold water and leave to soak for several hours.

Drain chestnuts, put in a saucepan and cover with cold water. Bring to the boil. Cover and simmer for 20-30 minutes or until chestnuts are tender. Drain and leave to cool. Bring a pan of water to the boil. Add rice and cook for 8-10 minutes until just tender. Drain and rinse with cold water. Preheat oven to 190C (375F/Gas 5). Chop chestnuts and pistachio nuts finely. Put in a bowl with rice, currants, salt, pepper and cinnamon. Mix well.

In a frying pan, melt butter. Add stuffing mixture. Cook, stirring, until thoroughly combined. Allow to cool. Stuff poussins with stuffing. Spread a little butter over each bird. Season with salt and pepper. Place in a roasting tin and roast, basting from time to time, for 45 minutes until thoroughly cooked and golden brown. Cut each poussin in half. Serve with the stuffing and pan juices.

Serves 4.

──GUINEA FOWL CASSEROLE──

55 ml (2 fl oz/¼ cup) olive oil
1 guinea fowl, cut into 4 pieces
1 large onion, finely sliced
1 clove garlic, crushed
400 g (14 oz) can chopped tomatoes
1 tablespoon chopped fresh oregano
salt and pepper
450 g (1 lb) small okra
halved black olives, to garnish

In a flameproof casserole, heat oil. Add guinea fowl pieces. Cook on both sides until brown. Transfer to a plate.

Add onion and garlic to casserole and cook until soft. Add tomatoes, oregano, 300 ml (10 fl oz/1¼ cups) water, salt and pepper. Bring to the boil, then add guinea fowl and coat well with sauce. Cover pan and simmer gently for 40 minutes.

Trim ends of okra without cutting pods. Put into a bowl of cold water; rinse gently and strain. Repeat until water is clear. Spread okra over guinea fowl. Cover and simmer for a further 30 minutes until okra is tender. Scatter black olives over the top and serve.

Serves 4.

SPICY GRILLED QUAIL

1 clove garlic
salt
1 teaspoon each ground cumin and coriander
½ small onion
1 tablespoon chopped fresh coriander
pinch cayenne pepper
55 ml (2 fl oz/¼ cup) olive oil
8 quail
vine leaves, parsley and lemon slices, to garnish

Put all the ingredients except quail and garnish in a food processor.

Process to make a paste. Spread paste over quail. Cover and leave to marinate in a cool place for 2 hours.

Grill quail for 10-15 minutes, turning frequently, until cooked and slightly charred on the outside. Serve quail on vine leaves, garnished with parsley and lemon slices.

Serves 4.

Variation: Baby poussins or chicken portions can be cooked in this way.

Note: The grilled quail are particularly good cooked on a barbecue.

——— POACHER'S PARTRIDGE ———

½ lemon
2 young partridges
4 sprigs thyme
4 sprigs oregano
2 bay leaves
2 cloves garlic
salt and pepper
6 rashers streaky bacon
olive oil
fresh herbs and lemon slices, to garnish
fried potatoes, to serve

Preheat oven to 170C (325F/Gas 3). Rub lemon over partridges.

Put 2 sprigs of thyme and oregano, a bay leaf and a clove of garlic in each bird. Season with salt and pepper. Wrap 3 rashers of bacon around each bird.

Brush 2 sheets foil with oil. Wrap partridges in foil. Place parcels in a baking tin. Bake in the oven for 1 hour until partridges are tender and juices run clear when the thickest part is pierced with a knife. Cut each partridge in half. Serve with the cooking juices poured over them, garnished with herbs and lemon slices, and accompanied by fried potatoes.

Serves 4.

RABBIT STIFADO

6 teaspoons plain flour
salt and pepper
700 g-1 kg (1½-2.2 lb) rabbit joints
70 ml (2½ fl oz/⅓ cup) olive oil
450 g (1 lb) tiny pickling onions, peeled
1 clove garlic, crushed
3 teaspoons tomato purée (paste)
300 ml (10 fl oz/1¼ cups) red wine
300 ml (10 fl oz/1¼ cups) chicken stock
1 bay leaf
2 sprigs thyme
2 slices bread, crusts removed, and 2 tablespoons
    chopped fresh parsley, to garnish

On a plate, mix together flour, salt and pepper. Toss rabbit pieces in seasoned flour. Heat half oil in a frying pan. Fry rabbit pieces until brown on both sides. Transfer to a flameproof casserole. Add onions to frying pan; cook until they begin to brown. Add garlic and tomato purée (paste) to pan and stir in wine and stock. Add bay leaf, thyme, salt and pepper. Add to casserole, cover and cook over a low heat for 1½-2 hours until rabbit is tender.

Cut each slice of bread into 4 triangles. In a frying pan, heat remaining oil and fry bread until golden brown on both sides. Dip one edge of each triangle into chopped parsley. To serve, place rabbit on a shallow plate and arrange onions around edge. Pour the sauce over the rabbit and garnish with fried bread.

Serves 6.

PITTA BREAD

800 g (1 ¾ lb/7 cups) strong white bread flour
1 sachet easy blend dried yeast
2 teaspoons salt
6 teaspoons olive oil

Sift flour into a large bowl. Stir in yeast and salt. Add oil and 425 ml (15 fl oz/scant 2 cups) tepid water. Mix together, then turn dough out onto a floured surface.

Knead dough thoroughly for 10 minutes until smooth and elastic. Cut into 12 equal pieces. Roll each piece into a ball, then roll out to an oval shape 18 cm (7 in) long. Place on floured trays; cover with a cloth; leave in a warm place for 1 hour or until puffed up to double the original size.

Preheat oven to 240C (475F/Gas 9). Oil 2 baking sheets and place in the oven to heat up. Place 3 pitta breads on each baking sheet and sprinkle with water. Bake in the oven for 5 minutes until puffed up and lightly browned. Remove from baking sheets and wrap in a cloth while baking remaining bread.

Makes 12.

OLIVE BREAD

70 ml (2½ fl oz/⅓ cup) olive oil
1 onion, finely chopped
800 g (1¾ lb/7 cups) strong white bread flour
1 sachet easy blend dried yeast
2 teaspoons salt
225 g (8 oz/1⅓ cups) black olives, stoned and chopped

In a frying pan, heat oil. Add onion and cook until soft. Leave to cool. Sift flour into a large bowl. Stir in yeast and salt. Add 6 teaspoons oil and 425 ml (15 fl oz/scant 1 cup) tepid water. Mix together, then turn dough onto a floured surface.

Knead dough thoroughly for 10 minutes until smooth and elastic. Knead in 3 teaspoons oil, the fried onion and chopped olives. Cut dough in half and shape into 2 round loaves. Place on lightly oiled baking sheets.

Cover with oiled plastic wrap and leave in a warm place for 1 hour or until doubled in size. Preheat oven to 180C (350F/Gas 4). Brush with a little of the oil. Bake loaves for 30-40 minutes until base of each sounds hollow when tapped. Brush tops of loaves with remaining oil. Return to the oven for 2 minutes, then transfer to wire racks to cool.

Makes 2 loaves.

CHEESE BUNS

800 g (1¾ lb/7 cups) strong white bread flour
1 sachet easy blend dried yeast
2 teaspoons salt
2 teaspoons caster sugar
6 teaspoons olive oil
sesame seeds, to decorate
CHEESE FILLING:
350 g (12 oz) kefalotiri cheese, grated
115 g (4 oz) haloumi cheese, finely grated
3 teaspoons plain flour
1 teaspoon baking powder
1 tablespoon chopped fresh mint
¼ teaspoon freshly grated nutmeg
4 eggs, beaten

To make the filling, place cheeses in a bowl.
Add flour, baking powder, mint and nutmeg
to cheese. Stir in most of beaten egg to make
a stiff paste. To make the dough, sift flour
into a bowl. Stir in yeast, salt and sugar. Add
oil and 425 ml (15 fl oz/scant 2 cups) tepid
water. Mix together, then turn dough onto a
floured surface and knead for 10 minutes until
smooth and elastic. Divide into 16 pieces;
roll out each piece to a 10 cm (4 in) circle.

Place a little filling in centre of each circle.
Pull dough up on 3 sides to make a tricorn
shape, with filling showing in centre. Pinch
corners together well. Place on oiled baking
sheets, cover with oiled plastic wrap and
leave in a warm place until doubled in size.
Preheat oven to 230C (450F/Gas 8). Brush
buns with remaining beaten egg. Scatter with
sesame seeds. Bake for 12-15 minutes until
golden brown.

Makes 16.

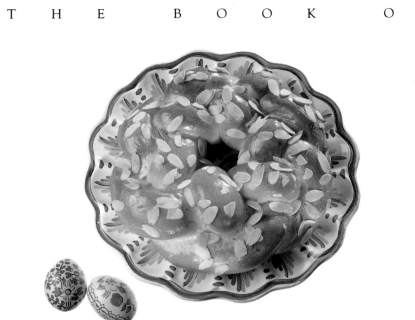

EASTER BREAD

800 g (1 ¾ lb/7 cups) strong white bread flour
1 sachet easy blend dried yeast
55 g (2 oz/¼ cup) caster sugar
2 teaspoons caraway seeds
115 g (4 oz/½ cup) butter, melted
2 eggs, beaten
225 ml (8 fl oz/1 cup) warm milk
1 egg, beaten, for glazing
6 teaspoons flaked almonds, to decorate

Sift flour into a large bowl. Stir in yeast, sugar and caraway seeds. Stir in butter, eggs and milk. Mix together, then turn dough out onto a floured surface.

Knead dough thoroughly for 10 minutes until smooth and elastic. Cut dough in half and divide each half into 3 pieces. Roll each piece into a rope 50 cm (20 in) long. Plait 3 ropes, then shape plait into a ring, pressing the ends together firmly. Repeat with remaining 3 ropes. Place the 2 rings on oiled baking sheets. Cover with a cloth and leave in a warm place for 1 hour or until doubled in size. Preheat oven to 190C (375F/Gas 5).

Brush loaves with beaten egg. Scatter flaked almonds over the top. Bake for 40 minutes or until loaves are lightly browned and sound hollow when tapped on the bases. Leave on wire racks to cool. Serve sliced and buttered.

Makes 2 loaves.

Note: Traditionally these loaves have red dyed eggs tucked into the braids before baking.

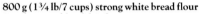

EASTER BISCUITS

55 g (2 oz/⅔ cup) walnuts
115 ml (4 fl oz/½ cup) sunflower oil
55 g (2 oz/¼ cup) caster sugar
25 g (1 oz/2 tablespoons) currants
1 egg
175 g (6 oz/1½ cups) plain flour
1 teaspoon baking powder
¼ teaspoon vanilla essence
icing sugar

Preheat oven to 180C (350F/Gas 4). Grease 2 baking sheets. In a food processor, chop walnuts finely. In a bowl, mix walnuts, sunflower oil, sugar, currants and egg.

Sift in flour and baking powder. Add vanilla essence. Stir together to form a firm paste, adding more flour if necessary.

Roll mixture into small walnut sized balls, flatten slightly and place on prepared baking sheets. Bake in the oven for 10 minutes or until crisp and golden. Transfer to wire racks to cool. Dust with icing sugar as they cool.

Makes about 14.

FESTIVAL CRESCENTS

130 g (4½ oz) hazelnuts
250 g (9 oz/1¼ cups) unsalted butter, softened
55 g (2 oz/¼ cup) caster sugar
1 egg yolk
2 tablespoons brandy
55 g (2 oz/½ cup) cornflour
300 g (10 oz/2½ cups) plain flour
orange flower water
icing sugar

In a food processor, chop nuts finely, without reducing to ground hazelnuts. Preheat oven to 180C (350F/Gas 4). Butter 2 or 3 baking sheets.

In a bowl, cream butter and caster sugar until pale and fluffy. Beat in egg yolk and brandy. Stir in hazelnuts. Sift cornflour and flour over mixture. Stir in, adding more flour, if necessary, to make a firm dough. With floured hands, break off small pieces of dough and roll into 7.5 cm (3 in) lengths, tapering into pointed ends. Shape into crescents; place on baking sheets. Bake for 20-25 minutes until firm; reduce heat if browning. Cool on wire racks.

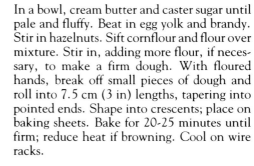

Pour orange flower water into a small bowl and icing sugar into a large one. Dip crescents very briefly into orange flower water, then into icing sugar, to coat completely. Pack loosely in a tin to avoid biscuits sticking together.

Makes about 40.

—— VANILLA RINGS ——

115 g (4 oz/½ cup) butter
85 g (3 oz/⅓ cup) caster sugar
½ teaspoon vanilla essence
1 egg yolk
175 g (6 oz/1½ cups) plain flour
½ teaspoon baking powder
1½ teaspoons ouzo
6 teaspoons chopped almonds

Preheat oven to 180C (350F/Gas 4). Grease 2 baking sheets. In a bowl, cream together butter and sugar until light and fluffy.

Beat in vanilla essence and egg yolk. Sift flour and baking powder over mixture, then add ouzo and mix to a smooth dough. Break off walnut sized pieces of dough.

Roll the pieces into short ropes and join the ends to make rings. Place on prepared baking sheets and scatter chopped almonds over the rings. Bake in the oven for 15-20 minutes until pale gold. Transfer to wire racks to cool.

Makes about 16.

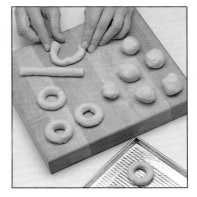

APRICOPITTA

1 kg (2.2 lb) fresh apricots
seeds from 5 cardamom pods
115 g (4 oz/½ cup) caster sugar
¼ teaspoon vanilla essence
85 g (3 oz/⅓ cup) butter, melted
12 sheets filo pastry
3 egg whites
45 g (1½ oz) demerara sugar
115 g (4 oz/1¼ cups) ground almonds
icing sugar

Put apricots in a bowl. Cover with boiling water. Leave for 2 minutes, then drain. Cover with cold water, leave for 2 minutes and drain again.

Peel skins off apricots. Cut in half and remove stones. Put apricots in a saucepan with cardamom seeds, caster sugar and vanilla essence. Cook gently until apricots are soft. In a blender or food processor, purée the apricots. Preheat oven to 190C (375F/Gas 5). Brush a small roasting tin with melted butter. Brush a sheet of pastry with butter and lay it in tin. Repeat with 3 more pastry layers. Spread apricot purée on pastry. Cover with 4 more layers of buttered pastry.

In a bowl, whisk egg whites until stiff. Whisk in demerara sugar. Fold in ground almonds. Spread meringue on pastry. Cover gently with 4 more sheets buttered pastry. Tuck top layer of pastry down sides. With a sharp knife, cut diamond shapes in pastry, down to meringue layer. Dust with icing sugar, then bake in oven for 40-50 minutes until browned and crisp. Serve warm or cold, cut into diamonds, and dusted with more sugar.

Serves 6-8.

BAKLAVA

115 g (4 oz/1 cup) blanched almonds
115 g (4 oz/1 cup) walnuts
55 g (2 oz/⅓ cup) shelled pistachio nuts
55 g (2 oz/⅓ cup) soft brown sugar
1 teaspoon ground cinnamon
¼ teaspoon freshly grated nutmeg
55 g (2 oz/¼ cup) butter
8 sheets filo pastry
SYRUP:
225 g (8 oz/1 cup) granulated sugar
1 tablespoon lemon juice
1 tablespoon orange flower water

To make syrup, in a saucepan, heat sugar, 150 ml (5 fl oz/⅔ cup) water and the lemon juice until sugar dissolves. Boil gently for 5 minutes until syrupy. Add orange flower water and boil for a further 2 minutes. Leave to cool completely. In a food processor, process one third of all nuts until finely chopped. Coarsely chop the remainder. In a bowl, mix together nuts, brown sugar, cinnamon and nutmeg. Butter a large baking tin. Preheat oven to 180C (350F/Gas 4). In a saucepan, melt butter.

Cut pastry sheets in half across. Brush one halved sheet with butter and place on bottom of baking tin. Repeat with 3 more sheets. Spread one third of nut mixture over the top, then repeat the layers twice more, ending with a layer of pastry. With a sharp knife, cut top layer of pastry into diamonds. Bake in oven for 30-40 minutes until crisp and golden. Pour cold syrup over the top. When cold, trim edges and cut into diamond shapes.

Makes about 20.

— CHEESE & HONEY TRIANGLES —

225 g (8 oz/1 cup) cream cheese
6 teaspoons set aromatic honey
1 egg yolk
55 g (2 oz/¼ cup) butter
6 sheets filo pastry
icing sugar for dusting

Preheat oven to 190C (375F/Gas 5). Butter a baking sheet. In a bowl, beat together cream cheese, honey and egg yolk.

In a small saucepan, melt butter. Brush a sheet of filo pastry with melted butter. Cover with a second sheet of pastry and brush with butter. Cover with a third sheet of pastry. Cut pastry layers in half across. Cut each half into 4 strips across. Repeat with remaining 3 sheets of pastry.

Place a spoonful of cream cheese mixture on corner of pastry strip. Fold pastry and filling over at right angles to make a triangle and continue folding in this way along strip of pastry to form a neat triangular parcel. Place on baking sheet and brush with melted butter. Repeat with remaining pastry strips and filling. Bake in the oven for 10 minutes until crisp. Dust lightly with icing sugar.

Makes 16.

WALNUT PASTRIES

300 g (10 fl oz/2 ½ cups) plain flour
175 g (6 oz/¾ cup) butter
85 g (3 oz/⅓ cup) icing sugar
1 egg yolk
9 teaspoons caster sugar
115 g (4 oz/1 cup) walnuts, coarsely chopped
85 g (3 oz/½ cup) chopped mixed citrus peel
¼ teaspoon freshly grated nutmeg
9 teaspoons rosewater
icing sugar for coating

Sift flour into a bowl. Rub in butter until mixture resembles breadcrumbs.

Sift in icing sugar and stir. Mix in egg yolk and a little water to make a firm dough. Chill for 30 minutes. Preheat oven to 180C (350F/ Gas 4). Butter a baking sheet. To make the syrup, in a saucepan, put caster sugar and 100 ml (3½ fl oz/⅓ cup) water. Heat gently until sugar has dissolved. Bring to the boil and boil for a few minutes until syrup has reduced and thickened slightly.

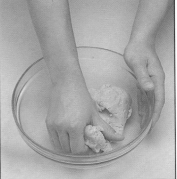

In a bowl, mix together walnuts, chopped mixed citrus peel and nutmeg. Moisten with the syrup. On a floured surface roll out pastry. Cut out 10 cm (4 in) circles. Place a teaspoon of walnut mixture on each circle. Fold in half, pressing edges together. Bake in the oven for 20-30 minutes until pale golden. Brush with rosewater. Coat liberally with icing sugar.

Makes about 20.

DIPLES

115 g (4 oz/1 cup) plain flour
½ teaspoon baking powder
6 teaspoons sunflower oil
2 eggs, beaten
grated rind ½ orange
sunflower oil for frying
9 teaspoons clear honey
chopped walnuts and ground cinnamon, to decorate

Sift flour and baking powder into a bowl. Stir in oil, eggs and orange rind. Mix to a firm dough, adding more flour if necessary. Chill for 30 minutes.

On a floured surface, roll out dough thinly. With a pastry wheel, cut into 2.5 cm x 12.5 cm (1 x 5 in) strips. Carefully tie into knots. Heat oil in a deep fat fryer and deep fry the knots, a few at a time. Drain on absorbent kitchen paper, then pile onto a serving dish.

In a small pan, heat honey, then pour it over the diples. Scatter chopped walnuts over the top and sprinkle with ground cinnamon.

Makes about 24.

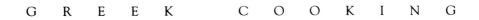

KADAIFI

115 g (4 oz/1 cup) finely chopped walnuts
115 g (4 oz/1 cup) finely chopped almonds
55 g (2 oz/¼ cup) caster sugar
½ teaspoon ground cinnamon
400 g (14 oz) kadaifi pastry (see Note)
55 g (2 oz/¼ cup) butter
SYRUP:
225 g (8 oz/1 cup) granulated sugar
3 teaspoons lemon juice
3 teaspoons orange flower water

Preheat oven to 180C (350F/Gas 4). Butter a
baking tray. In a bowl, mix together walnuts,
almonds, sugar and cinnamon.

Tease pastry out to a rectangle 45 x 37.5 cm
(18 x 15 in). Cut into 18 pieces measuring
12.5 x 7.5 cm (5 x 3 in). Place 1 tablespoon
of nut mixture on short end of each rectangle
of pastry. Roll up, enclosing filling. Place
rolls on the baking tray. In a small saucepan,
melt butter, then pour it over the rolls. Bake
in the oven for 25-30 minutes until golden
and crisp. Leave to cool for 15 minutes.

To make the syrup, put sugar, the lemon juice
and 300 ml (10 fl oz/1¼ cups) water in a
saucepan. Heat gently until sugar has dissolved, then boil for 5 minutes until slightly
thickened. Add orange flower water, then
pour syrup over pastry rolls.

Makes 18.

Note: Kadaifi is a white shredded raw pastry
available from delicatessens and Greek
shops. It has to be teased into shape rather
than rolled.

HONEY CAKES

225 g (8 oz/2 cups) plain flour
½ teaspoon ground cinnamon
¼ teaspoon ground cloves
¼ teaspoon freshly grated nutmeg
55 g (2 oz/¼ cup) caster sugar
6 teaspoons dry white wine
6 teaspoons ouzo
juice ½ orange
3 teaspoons brandy
115 ml (4 fl oz/½ cup) sunflower oil
chopped almonds and ground cinnamon, to decorate
SYRUP:
115 ml (4 fl oz/½ cup) clear honey
115 g (4 oz/½ cup) caster sugar
6 teaspoons lemon juice

Preheat oven to 200C (400F/Gas 6). Grease a baking sheet. Sift flour, cinnamon, cloves and nutmeg into a mixing bowl. Stir in sugar. In a separate bowl, mix together wine, ouzo, orange juice and brandy. Stir oil into flour, then gradually beat in other liquids until a stiff dough is formed. Add more flour if necessary. Break off pieces the size of a large walnut. Form into balls, place on baking sheet and press to flatten slightly. Bake in the oven for 15 minutes until brown.

Meanwhile, make the syrup. In a saucepan, put honey, sugar, lemon juice and 115 ml (4 fl oz/½ cup) water. Heat gently until sugar is dissolved. Bring to the boil and boil until mixture is frothy. While cakes are still warm, dip them into syrup for 2 minutes. Place on wire racks. Scatter chopped almonds over the top and sprinkle with ground cinnamon.

Makes about 14.

HALVA CAKE

115 g (4 oz/½ cup) butter
115 g (4 oz/½ cup) caster sugar
grated rind 1 orange
juice ½ lemon
2 eggs, beaten
175 g (6 oz/1 cup) semolina
2 teaspoons baking powder
100 g (3½ oz/1 cup) ground almonds
1 teaspoon ground cinnamon
SYRUP:
175 g (6 oz/¾ cup) caster sugar
juice ½ lemon
juice ½ orange
6 teaspoons candied orange peel, to decorate

Preheat oven to 220C (425F/Gas 7). Butter a ring mould. In a blender or food processor, put butter, sugar, orange rind, lemon juice, eggs, semolina, baking powder, ground almonds and cinnamon. Process until well mixed. Turn mixture into prepared tin. Bake in the oven for 10 minutes, then reduce heat to 180C (350F/Gas 4) and bake for a further 25 minutes or until a skewer inserted into the cake comes out clean. Leave to cool in the tin for a few minutes, then turn out into a warm, deep plate.

Meanwhile, make the syrup. In a pan, put sugar, lemon juice, orange juice and 115 ml (4 fl oz/½ cup) water. Heat gently until sugar has dissolved, then bring to the boil and simmer for 4 minutes. Stir in candied peel. As soon as cake is turned out, bring syrup to the boil; spoon over cake so that peel is arranged decoratively over the cake.

Serves 8.

ARTEMIS CAKE

400 g (14 oz) plain (dark) chocolate
5 eggs, separated
225 g (8 oz/1 cup) butter, softened
115 g (4 oz/¾ cup) icing sugar, sifted
6 teaspoons plain flour, sifted
1 teaspoon ground cinnamon
icing sugar, to decorate

Preheat oven to 180C (350F/Gas 4). Butter
and line a 20 cm (8 in) cake tin (preferably a
loose-bottomed tin). Break chocolate into a
bowl and stand bowl over a pan of hot water
until melted. Leave until almost cold.

In a bowl, whisk egg whites until stiff. In a
bowl, beat butter and icing sugar until light
and creamy. Beat in egg yolks. Add chocolate; stir in lightly. It does not need to be
thoroughly mixed.

Stir in flour and cinnamon and then fold in
whisked egg whites. Pour mixture into prepared tin. Bake in the oven for 45 minutes
until well risen and firm to the touch. Leave
in tin until almost cool, then transfer to a
wire rack. Sift icing sugar over the top and
place on a serving plate.

Serves 8.

YOGURT CAKE

4 eggs, separated
225 g (8 oz/1½ cups) caster sugar
115 ml (4 fl oz/½ cup) sunflower oil
¼ teaspoon bicarbonate of soda
225 ml (8 fl oz/1 cup) yogurt
grated rind ½ lemon
300 g (10 oz/2½ cups) plain flour
3 teaspoons baking powder
icing sugar and lemon rind, to decorate

Preheat oven to 190C (375F/Gas 5). Grease
and line a 23 cm (9 in) cake tin. In a bowl,
whisk egg yolks and sugar until creamy.

Gradually mix in oil. Stir bicarbonate of soda
into yogurt. Stir yogurt and lemon rind into
egg yolk mixture. Sift flour and baking
powder into mixture and fold in carefully.
Beat egg whites until standing in peaks and
fold in.

Pour mixture into prepared tin. Bake in the
oven for 40-50 minutes until well risen, and a
skewer inserted into the centre comes out
clean. Leave in tin for 5 minutes, then
transfer to a wire rack to cool. Dust with icing
sugar and scatter lemon rind over the top.

Serves 8-10.

LAVENDER & HONEY ICE CREAM

5 sprigs lavender flowers
550 ml (20 fl oz/2½ cups) milk
175 g (6 oz/¾ cup) lavender honey
4 egg yolks
150 ml (5 fl oz/⅔ cup) double (heavy) cream
150 ml (5 fl oz/⅔ cup) yogurt
lavender flowers, to decorate

Turn freezer to its coldest setting. In a saucepan, heat lavender sprigs and milk to almost boiling. Remove from heat and leave to infuse for 30 minutes. Remove lavender sprigs and bring milk back to the boil.

In a small saucepan, heat honey until just melted. In a bowl, whisk egg yolks until thick and light. Gradually add melted honey. Pour boiling milk onto egg yolk mixture, beating constantly. Pour mixture into a bowl set over a pan of boiling water. Stir for about 8 minutes until custard will coat the back of the spoon. Strain into a bowl, cover and leave to cool. Stir in cream and yogurt.

Pour mixture into an 850 ml (30 fl oz/3¾ cup) freezerproof container. Put in freezer. When sides are beginning to set, beat thoroughly. Return to freezer and repeat after 30-40 minutes. When ice cream is just beginning to solidify, beat vigorously to a smooth slush. Return to freezer. Transfer from freezer to refrigerator 20 minutes before serving. Decorate with lavender flowers.

Serves 4-6.

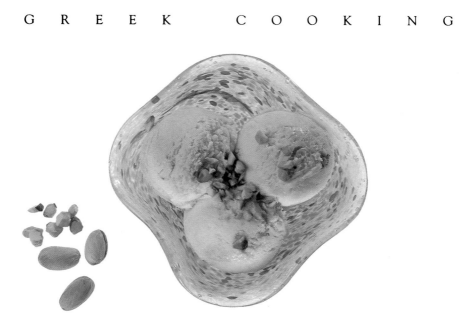

– PISTACHIO HALVA ICE CREAM –

3 eggs yolks
115 g (4 oz/½ cup) caster sugar
300 ml (10 fl oz/1¼ cups) single (light) cream
300 ml (10 fl oz/1¼ cups) double (heavy) cream
115 g (4 oz) pistachio halva
chopped pistachio nuts, to decorate

Turn freezer to its lowest setting. In a bowl, whisk together egg yolks and sugar until thick and pale. In a small saucepan, bring single (light) cream to the boil, pour onto egg yolk mixture and mix well.

Transfer to double boiler or bowl placed over a pan of boiling water. Cook, stirring constantly, until thick enough to coat the back of a spoon. Strain into a bowl and leave to cool. In a bowl, whip double (heavy) cream lightly, then whisk in custard. Crumble halva into mixture and stir in gently.

Pour into a freezerproof container. Cover and freeze for 3 hours or until half set. Stir well, then return to freezer until frozen. Remove from freezer 15 minutes before serving. Decorate with chopped pistachio nuts.

Serves 6.

DRIED FRUIT SALAD

115 g (4 oz/¾ cup) soft brown sugar
6 teaspoons rosewater
225 g (8 oz) dried apricots
225 g (8 oz) dates
225 g (8 oz) dried figs
115 g (4 oz/¾ cup) raisins
115 g (4 oz/¾ cup) split almonds
55 g (2 oz) pistachio nuts
yogurt, to serve

In a bowl, put sugar and 150 ml (5 fl oz/ ⅔ cup) warm water. Stir until sugar has dissolved. Stir in the rosewater and 425 ml (15 fl oz/2 cups) cold water. Add apricots, dates, figs and raisins to bowl. Stir and turn them in the liquid, adding more water, if necessary, to cover.

Cover bowl and leave in a cold place for at least 24 hours. When ready to serve, add almonds and pistachio nuts and stir to mix with the fruit. Serve with yogurt.

Serves 6-8.

FRUIT PLATTER

1 small melon
2 peaches
4 figs
175 g (6 oz) seedless green grapes
orange flower water
2 pomegranates

Halve melon and remove seeds. Cut into thin slices and remove skin. Arrange slices on 4 plates.

Put peaches in a bowl and pour boiling water over. Leave for 30 seconds, then plunge into cold water for 30 seconds. Peel off skins. Cut peaches in half and remove stones. Cut into slices and arrange on the plates. Cut figs into slices and add to the plates. Arrange grapes on the plates.

Sprinkle the fruit with orange flower water. Cut pomegranates in half and scoop out seeds, removing any pith. Scatter the seeds over the fruit on the plates.

Serves 4.

CUSTARD PIES

2 eggs, separated
115 g (4 oz/½ cup) caster sugar
55 g (2 oz/⅓ cup) semolina
550 ml (20 fl oz/2½ cups) milk
85 g (3 oz/⅓ cup) butter
8 sheets filo pastry
icing sugar and ground cinnamon, to decorate

In a bowl, beat together egg yolks, sugar, semolina and a little of the milk until creamy.

In a saucepan, heat remaining milk until almost boiling. Gradually whisk milk into egg mixture. Return to saucepan. Cook gently, stirring, for 5 minutes until mixture thickens. Stir in a knob of butter. Cover surface closely with plastic wrap. Leave until cold. In a bowl, whisk egg whites until holding peaks. Fold into custard. Preheat oven to 200C (400F/Gas 6). Butter a baking sheet.

In a small pan, melt remaining butter. Brush a sheet of pastry with butter. Place another sheet on top; brush with butter. Repeat with 2 more sheets. Cut pastry into 12 squares. Put a little custard mixture in middle of each square. Draw edges of pastry together to form a pouch. Pinch 'neck' firmly together. Repeat with remaining pastry and filling. Place pies on baking sheets. Bake in the oven for 15 minutes until golden brown. Dust with icing sugar and cinnamon.

Makes 24.

HONEY CHEESECAKES

3 teaspoons raisins
3 teaspoons orange flower water
225 g (8 oz/1 cup) cream cheese
9 teaspoons orange blossom honey
2 small eggs, beaten
mint leaves, to decorate
PASTRY:
150 g (5 oz/1¼ cups) plain flour
85 g (3 oz/⅓ cup) butter
9 teaspoons icing sugar
1 egg yolk
CARAMELISED ORANGE PEEL:
115 g (4 oz/½ cup) caster sugar
25 g (1 oz) orange peel, cut into julienne strips

Put raisins and orange flower water in a small bowl to soak. Make the pastry. Sift flour into a bowl. Rub in butter until mixture resembles breadcrumbs. Stir in icing sugar. Mix in egg yolk and a little water to make a firm dough. Chill for 30 minutes. Make the candied orange peel. Put sugar and 100 ml (3½ fl oz/⅓ cup) water into a saucepan. Heat gently until sugar is dissolved. Bring to the boil and boil for 2 minutes. Blanch orange peel for 2-3 minutes in boiling water. Drain, add to syrup and cook for 20 minutes until peel is transparent.

Preheat oven to 180C (350F/Gas 4). On a floured surface, roll pastry thinly. Use to line 4 deep loose-bottomed 10 cm (4 in) tart tins. In a bowl, beat together raisins, cream cheese, honey and eggs. Pour into pastry cases. Bake in the oven for 25-30 minutes until set and golden. Decorate with candied orange peel and mint leaves.

Makes 4.

RIZOGALO

85 g (3 oz/½ cup) rice
550 ml (20 fl oz/2½ cups) milk
piece lemon peel
55 g (2 oz/¼ cup) caster sugar
1½ teaspoons cornflour
1 egg yolk, beaten
2 teaspoons rosewater
ground cinnamon and rose petals, to decorate
   (optional)

Wash rice. Put in a bowl with 115 ml (4 fl oz/
½ cup) water.

In a saucepan, put milk and lemon peel and
bring to the boil. Add sugar and stir until
dissolved. Add rice and the water. Simmer
gently, covered, for 30-40 minutes until most
of the milk has been absorbed.

Mix cornflour with a little water, add to rice
and cook for a further 2-3 minutes, stirring.
Stir in egg yolk and cook gently for 2-3
minutes, stirring. Stir in rosewater. Pour into
serving dishes and leave to cool. Decorate
with ground cinnamon, then scatter rose
petals over the top, if desired.

Serves 4.

——ORANGES & WALNUTS——

4 oranges
1 teaspoon orange flower water
115 g (4 oz) dates
55 g (2 oz/²⁄₃ cup) walnuts
mint leaves, to decorate

Carefully cut skins off oranges, removing any pith. Cut oranges into segments by cutting down between the membranes. Reserve any juice in a bowl.

Arrange the segments on a serving plate. Pour reserved juice over the top and then sprinkle with orange flower water.

Remove stones from dates. Chop dates and walnuts. Scatter them over the oranges. Serve decorated with mint leaves.

Serves 4.

INDEX